NTC's
Dictionary
of
EVERYDAY
AMERICAN
ENGLISH
EXPRESSIONS

D0980628

NTC's Dictionary

of

EVERYDAY AMERICAN ENGLISH EXPRESSIONS

Presented According to Topic and Situation

Richard A. Spears, Ph.D.
Steven R. Kleinedler, B.A.
Betty J. Birner, Ph.D.

McGraw·Hill

New York   Chicago   San Francisco   Lisbon   London   Madrid   Mexico City
Milan   New Delhi   San Juan   Seoul   Singapore   Sydney   Toronto

Library of Congress Cataloging-in-Publication Data

Spears, Richard A.
    NTC's dictionary of everyday American English expressions : presented
according to topic and situation / Richard A. Spears, Stephen R. Kleinedler, Betty J. Birner.
       p.   cm.
    ISBN 0-8442-5779-6 (paperback)
     1. English language—United States—Terms and phrases.   2. English language—
Spoken English—United States.   3. English language—United States—Idioms.
4. Figures of speech.   5. Americanisms.   I. Kleinedler, Steven Racek.
II. Birner, Betty J.   III. Title: Dictionary of everyday American English expressions.
IV. Title.   V. Series: National Textbook language dictionaries.

PE2839 .S65   1994
423'.1—dc20   95-139741

Copyright © 1994 by The McGraw-Hill Companies, Inc. All rights reserved. Printed in the
United States of America. Except as permitted under the United States Copyright Act of 1976,
no part of this publication may be reproduced or distributed in any form or by any means, or
stored in a database or retrieval system, without the prior written permission of the publisher.

16 17 18 19 20 21 22 23 WFR / WFR 0

ISBN 0-8442-5779-6 (paperback)

McGraw-Hill books are available at special quantity discounts to use as premiums and sales
promotions, or for use in corporate training programs. For more information, please write to
the Director of Special Sales, Professional Publishing, McGraw-Hill, Two Penn Plaza, New York,
NY 10121-2298. Or contact your local bookstore.

This book is printed on acid-free paper.

CONTENTS

ABOUT THIS DICTIONARY

Every language has conventional and much used ways of expressing even the most commonplace requests, inquiries, or responses. Some of these expressions are idioms or idiomatic. Others are perfectly understandable and literal English, but people unfamiliar with the language may have difficulty formulating them in typical and conventional ways. This book is a collection of more than 7,000 such **expressions** grouped into 774 **topics** that are listed under 18 **major categories** of social interaction.

The complete list of major category headings and their topics can be found in the **Topic and Situation Index,** beginning on page 3. This index can also be used for browsing through the topics. See a complete explanation of how to use this index on page 1. Each of the 774 topics has been assigned a number and it is this number that is the basis of the indexing systems. These numbers appear at the top of each page of the body of the book to aid in finding a particular topic.

The **Word and Concept Index** allows the user to locate a particular topic based on a key word or concept that is part of the topic. See a complete explanation of how to use this index on page 337.

USING THIS DICTIONARY

The meaning of the expressions can be determined from the topic heading. All the expressions under a particular heading convey essentially the same type of information.

- The expressions themselves contain hints and explanations where necessary. For instance, in the expression . . .

I got sidetracked.
   sidetracked = detoured; distracted

. . . the equal sign (=) indicates that the word or phrase on the left is defined as the word or phrase on the right.

- In the expression . . .

Can you stay for dinner?
   Can you ≈ Would you, Are you able to, Will you

. . . the ≈ indicates that the word or phrase on the left can be replaced by any of the words or phrases on the right.

- In the expression . . .

Get off your high horse. *(informal)*
   = Be less arrogant.

. . . the equal sign (=) at the beginning of the line indicates that a restatement of the entire expression follows.

- In the expression . . .

You and what army? *(slang)*

. . . the word *slang* in parenthesis indicates the register or usage of the expression. Other similar indicators are *Biblical, cliché, euphemistic, folksy, formal, French, German, idiomatic, informal, ironic, Italian, Japanese, jocular, juvenile, Latin, mild oath, mildly vulgar, oath, rude, sarcastic, Spanish, taboo,* and *vulgar.*

• In the expression . . .

Fore!

> *(said in golfing when the ball is struck)*

. . . the information in parenthesis explains something about the context in which the expression is used.

• In the expression . . .

Good things come to **him** who waits. (Cliché.)

. . . the boldface type indicates that only the pronoun shown may be used correctly in the expression. A pronoun having the opposite gender may not be substituted.

TOPIC AND SITUATION INDEX

Basic Social Encounters • Conversational Encounters

Polite Encounters • Impolite Encounters • Visits

Miscellaneous Expressions • Personal Matters

Family Matters • Money Matters • Food and Drink

Health • Employment • Shopping • Service Encounters

Telephones • Travel and Transportation

Lodging • Emergencies

Using the Topic and Situation Index

The book includes eighteen major category headings, under which the topics for each category appear in boldface type. The specific expression groups for each topic are then presented in the order in which they are found in the list of expressions. A topic number, rather than a page number, is provided at the end of each topic description, indicating where to find that topic in the list of expressions.

For instance, if you wanted to find an expression having to do with a pain in the head, you would look under the category **HEALTH** for a group of expressions labeled **Sickness.** Under **sickness** you would find the expression group "Describing a pain in the head **488**." Look for "Describing a pain in the head" at number 488 in the list of expressions.

TOPIC AND SITUATION INDEX

BASIC SOCIAL ENCOUNTERS

Agreeing

Disagreeing

CONVERSATIONAL ENCOUNTERS

Focusing Attention

Launching the Conversation

Making Friends

POLITE ENCOUNTERS

Special Occasions

IMPOLITE ENCOUNTERS

Dealing with Unpleasantness

VISITS

MISCELLANEOUS EXPRESSIONS

Comments and Phrases

PERSONAL MATTERS

FAMILY MATTERS

MONEY MATTERS

EMPLOYMENT

SHOPPING

Stores and Shops

Shoe Repair Shops

Drugstores

The Post Office

The Tailor

Tickets

Florists

Newspapers and Magazines

Automobiles

SERVICE ENCOUNTERS

Babysitters

TELEPHONES

TRAVEL AND TRANSPORTATION

Travel Agents

Air Travel

Railway Travel

Long-Distance Bus Travel

Local Bus and Subway Travel

LODGING

Hotels

Rooms and Apartments

EMERGENCIES

Accidents

Using 911, The Emergency Telephone Number

The Life and Death Emergency

NTC's
Dictionary
of
EVERYDAY
AMERICAN
ENGLISH
EXPRESSIONS

BASIC SOCIAL ENCOUNTERS

GREETINGS

1   **Simple greetings**

Hi!

Hello!

Hello there!

Howdy!

Hey!

Yo! (*slang*)

2   **General greetings**

How are you?

How's it going?

How's it been?

How is everything?

How's everything?

How have you been?

How've you been?

How you been? (*informal*)

How's tricks? (*informal*)

What have you been up to?

What's new? (*informal*)

What's up? (*informal*)

What's happening? (*slang*)

What's going on? (*slang*)

3   **Greetings for various times of the day**

Good morning.

Morning.

Mornin'. (*informal*)

How are you this bright morning?

Good afternoon.

Afternoon.

Good evening.

Evening.

4   Greeting a person you haven't seen in a long time

I haven't seen you in years!

Long time no see! (*informal*)

I haven't seen you in an age!

I haven't seen you in a month of Sundays!

   a month of Sundays = a long time

5   Expressing surprise at meeting someone

What a surprise to meet you here!

Imagine meeting you here! (*cliché*)

Fancy meeting you here. (*cliché*)

Never thought I'd see you here!

What are you doing in this neck of the woods?

   neck of the woods = part of town; location

What are you doing in this part of town?

What are you doing out of the office?

Where've you been hiding yourself?

What have you been up to?

Shouldn't you be in school?

Shouldn't you be at work?

Have you been keeping busy?

You been keeping busy?

Been keeping busy?

Have you been keeping cool?

You been keeping cool?

6   After you have greeted someone

We seem to keep running into each other.

Haven't we met before?

We have to stop meeting like this. (*cliché*)

Didn't we meet at that party last week?

I'm sorry; I've forgotten your name.

I've been meaning to call you.

SMALL TALK

7   Expressing your state of health and happiness

Fine.

I'm fine.

I'm cool. (*slang*)

Keeping cool.

Dandy. (*informal*)

Fine and dandy.

Great.

Couldn't be better.

Happy as a clam. (*cliché*)

Okay.

All right.

(I) can't complain.

No complaints.

I have nothing to complain about.

8   Telling how you have been doing — positive

Keeping busy.

Keeping myself busy.

Been keeping myself busy.

Keeping out of trouble.

Been keeping out of trouble.

Been up to no good. (*informal*)

Been keeping my nose clean. (*informal*)

9 Telling how you have been doing — neutral

Getting by.

Been getting by.

Fair to middling. (*folksy*)

So-so. (*informal*)

Plugging along. (*informal*)

Could be worse.

Could be better.

(Just) muddling through.

Same as always.

Same as usual.

10 Telling how you have been doing — negative

Not good.

Not so good.

Not too good.

None too good.

Not well.

Not very well.

Not so well.

Not too well.

None too well.

Not so hot.

Not too hot.

None too hot.

Not great.

Not so great.

None too great.

Crummy. (*slang*)

Kind of crummy. (*slang*)

Lousy. (*slang*)

I've seen better days.

I've had better days.

Could be better.

I've been better.

I've been under the weather.

11 Explaining that you have been busy

I'm busy.

Keeping busy.

Keeping myself busy.

Been keeping myself busy.

I'm swamped.

> *swamped = overwhelmed, as with a swamped boat*

I'm snowed under.

> *snowed under = as if buried in snow*

I don't have time to breathe.

I don't have time to think.

There aren't enough hours in the day.

Not a moment to spare.

I've been running around with my head cut off. (*informal*)

I've been running around like a chicken with its head cut off. (*informal*)

12 Inviting a friend for a drink or coffee

Do you have time for coffee?

How about a cup of coffee?

Let's go get coffee. Do you have any time?

Let's go for coffee.

Let's go for a beer.

Let's go for a drink.

INTRODUCTIONS

13 Introducing someone to someone else

I'd like you to meet my friend Mary.

I'd like you to meet Mary.

This is my friend Mary.

John, (this is) Mary. Mary, John.

Mary, have you met John?

Mary, do you know John?

Mary, shake hands with John Jones.

Do you two know each other?

Have you met?

Have you two been introduced?

Haven't you been introduced?

Oh, I'm sorry; how silly of me. This is Mary.

Mary, John is the guy I was telling you about. (*informal*)

You two have a lot in common.

14 When you have just been introduced to someone

Good to meet you.

Nice to meet you.

Nice meeting you.

How nice to meet you. (*formal*)

How very nice to meet you. (*formal*)

What a pleasure to meet you. (*formal*)

It's a pleasure to have finally met you. (*formal*)

I am pleased to make your acquaintance. (*formal*)

I'm happy to meet you.

I'm glad to meet you.

Glad to meet you.

Charmed. (*formal*)

A pleasure. (*formal*)

15 After you have been introduced to someone

I've been wanting to meet you for some time.

John has told me all about you.

John has told me so much about you.

I've heard so much about you.

I've heard so much about you I feel I know you already.
So we finally meet face-to-face.
I'm sorry, what was your name again?
I didn't catch your name. I'm terrible at names.

16 Asking how someone is

How are you?
How's your family?
How's the family?
How are you doing?
How are you doing today?
How you doing?
Are you doing OK?
How are you feeling?
How you feeling?
Are you feeling better today?
How have you been?
How you been?

17 Asking someone how things are going

How're things?
How're things with you?
How're things going?
How's with you?
How's by you? (*slang*)
How's business?
How's tricks? (*slang*)
How's it shakin'? (*slang*)
How's everything?
How's every little thing? (*folksy*)
How's everything going?
How's it going?
How goes it?

How goes it with you?

How are you getting on?

How are you getting along?

How's the world (been) treating you?

ENDING A CONVERSATION

18 **Signaling the end of a conversation**

Oh, look at the time!

It's getting later.

Well, Tom, it's really good to see you, but I really must go.

It's been fun talking to you.

(It's been) nice chatting with you.

It's so good to see you again.

We have to make plans to get together sometime.

Let's do lunch sometime.

19 **Ending a telephone conversation**

I really have to go now. We'll talk sometime.

There's someone on the other line. I must say good-bye now.

The doorbell is ringing. I'll call you back.

Can I call you back? Something has come up.

I have to get back to my work. I'll call again later.

Can we continue this later? My other line is ringing.

I have to get back to work before the boss sees me.

I won't keep you any longer.

I'll let you go now.

20 **Ending a conversation abruptly**

I'm going to have to run.

I'm all out of time. I'll have to say good-bye now.

Look at the time. I really must go.

It's been great talking to you, but I have to go.

Wow! I'm late. Look, I'll call you.

Sorry, but I have to leave now.

Let's continue this another time. I really must go.

GOOD-BYES

21   **Simple good-byes**

Good-bye.

Bye.

Bye-bye.

So long.

Ta-ta. (*informal*)

Farewell.

Cheerio.

Hasta la vista. (*Spanish*)

Adios. (*Spanish*)

Auf wiedersehen. (*German*)

Sayonara. (*Japanese*)

Arrivederci. (*Italian*)

Au revoir. (*French*)

Adieu. (*French*)

Ciao. (*Italian*)

Good day. (*formal*)

Good evening. (*formal*)

Good night.

Good-bye until later.

Good-bye until next time.

Good-bye for now.

See you later.

See you later, alligator. (*slang*)

Later, gator. (*slang*)

Later. (*informal*)

I'll try to catch you later.

I'll catch you later.

Catch you later.

I'll talk to you soon.

Let's get together soon.

I'll be seeing you.

I'll see you real soon.

See you.

See ya. (*informal*)

See you soon.

See you real soon.

See you around.

See you in a little while.

See you next year.

See you then.

See you tomorrow.

22   Taking leave of someone

Good running into you.

> *running into you = meeting up with you*

Nice running into you.

Nice talking to you.

Take care.

(It was) good to see you.

(It was) nice to see you.

Nice meeting you.

It was a pleasure meeting you. (*formal*)

It is a pleasure to have met you. (*formal*)

It's been a real pleasure. (*formal*)

23   Leaving a place

Are we ready to leave?

Are you about finished?

Are you ready to go?

Ready to go?

Ready to roll? (*slang*)

Are we away? (*slang*)

Let's blow. (*slang*)

    blow = leave

Let's blow this pop(sicle) stand. (*slang*)

    pop(sicle) stand = a cheap place; an undesirable place

Let's get out of this taco stand. (*slang*)

    taco stand = a cheap place; an undesirable place

Let's blow this joint. (*slang*)

    = Let's leave this place.

Let's go while the going's good. (*cliché*)

    Let's ≈ Time to, We got to

Let's get while the getting's good. (*cliché*)

Let's head out.

Let's beat a hasty retreat. (*cliché*)

Let's make tracks. (*informal*)

    make tracks = leave a trail (as we go)

Let's motor. (*slang*)

    to motor = to leave by automobile

Let's hit the road. (*slang*)

Let's boogie. (*slang*)

Let's split. (*slang*)

Let's make like a tree and leave. (*jocular*)

Let's make like the wind and blow. (*jocular*)

Let's make like a banana and split. (*jocular*)

Exit stage right.

Exit stage left.

Retreat! (*slang*)

24   Making plans to keep in touch with someone

I'll call you when I get home.

Call when you get there.

Don't forget to call.
Write me.
Let's write.
Let's do lunch.
I'll be in touch.
Let's keep in touch.

AGREEING

25 **Simple agreement**
Yes.
Yeah. (*informal*)
Yep. (*informal*)
Yup. (*informal*)
Right.
You're right.
Right you are.
Right on!
Right-o.
Uh-huh.
Sure.
You got it.
You bet.
Absolutely.
By all means.

26 **Stating your concurrence**
This is true.
That's true.
You're right.
Ain't that the truth?
Ain't it the truth?
That's right.
That's for certain.

That's for sure.

That's for darn sure.

That's for damn sure. (*mildly vulgar*)

Damn straight! (*mildly vulgar*)

It works for me.

Well said.

I agree.

I agree with you 100%.

I couldn't agree with you more.

I have no problem with that.

We see eye to eye on this.

I couldn't have said it better.

You took the words right out of my mouth.

I'll drink to that!

27 Expressing acceptance

It's fine.

I think it's fine.

It's good enough.

It's satisfactory.

It'll do.

It'll serve the purpose.

I like it.

I love it.

I think it's great.

I like the color.

I like the texture.

I like the flavor.

It's got a good rhythm.

It's wonderful.

It's fabulous.

It's ideal.

It's a masterpiece.

It's perfect.

It's A-1.

This is second to none.

This is perfect.

This is far and away the best.

This is the ultimate.

It couldn't be better.

Never been better.

There's none better.

It doesn't get any better than this.

I've never seen anything like it.

This is the cream of the crop. (*cliché*)

This is the pick of the litter. (*idiomatic*)

>   *litter = a group of newborn pups*

This is the crème de la crème. (*cliché*)

>   = *This is the best of the best.*

This is head and shoulders above the rest.

That suits me to a T.

>   = *That suits me fine.*

That's the ticket. (*idiomatic*)

That's just what the doctor ordered. (*idiomatic*)

That's just what I needed.

That hits the spot. (*idiomatic*)

That fits the bill. (*idiomatic*)

That's it.

That's the greatest thing since sliced bread. (*cliché*)

It's in a league of its own.

I give it four stars.

It gets two thumbs up. (*idiomatic*)

I've hit the jackpot.

>   *jackpot = sum of money to be won in gambling*

Bingo! (*slang*)

>   = *I did it!*

Jackpot! (*slang*)
   = *I did it!; It is good!*
Bull's-eye! (*slang*)
Bonus! (*slang*)

28   Stating that you understand
I hear you.
I hear you, man.
I hear what you're saying.
I see what you're saying.
I can see what you're saying.
I can see that.
I see what you mean.
I see where you're coming from.
I know.
I know what you mean.
Point well-taken.
I know what you're talking about.
I understand what you're saying.
Understood.
I dig it. (*slang*)
I can dig it. (*slang*)
I got you.
Gotcha.
(I) got it.
I follow you.
I'm with you.
I'm there with you.
I've been there.
Read you loud and clear.
Roger.
Roger, wilco.
   wilco = will comply
Roger Dodger. (*slang*)

29 Making sure you are understood

Do you know what I mean?

Do you know what I'm talking about?

Know what I mean?

Does that make any sense?

Am I making sense?

Are you following me?

Know what I'm saying?

You know?

Do you see what I mean?

See what I mean?

Don't you see?

Do you get the message?

Do you get the picture?

Get the message?

Get the picture?

Get my drift?

Do you get it?

Get it?

Do you follow?

Do you follow me?

Dig? (*slang*)

    = *Do you understand?*

Understand?

Do you understand?

Do you hear what I'm saying?

Do you hear me?

Do you see where I'm coming from?

    where I'm coming from = what my position is

Do you agree?

You're with me, right?

Are you with me on this?

Do we see eye to eye on this?

DISAGREEING

30   Stating simple disagreement or refusal

No.

Nope.

No way.

Not a chance.

Not! (*slang*)

Uh-uh.

I don't think so.

31   Stating categorical disagreement

That's not true.

That's not right.

You've got that wrong.

You've got it all wrong.

Wrong!

You missed the boat. (*idiomatic*)

You're missing the boat. (*idiomatic*)

Wrong on both counts.

You're wrong.

You're dead wrong.

You're off.

You're way off base.

32   Stating strong disagreement

I disagree completely.

I couldn't disagree (with you) more.

Horsefeathers!

Bullshit. (*taboo*)

Bull. (*mildly vulgar*)

Baloney. (*slang*)

That's a load of crap. (*mildly vulgar*)

That's a lot of bull. (*mildly vulgar*)

That's a lot of baloney. (*slang*)

That's a bunch of baloney. (*slang*)
That's a bunch of malarkey.
Lies!
That's a lie.
That's a big, fat lie. (*informal*)
You're lying through your teeth.
Look me in the eye and say that.

33 Stating your disagreement with a proposition
That's out of the question.
That's unthinkable.
That's insane.
That doesn't even merit a response.
I'll give that all the consideration it's due.

34 Expressing rejection
I can't stand it.
I hate it.
I don't care for it.
I don't like it.
It's not my style.
It's not for me.
It stinks. (*informal*)
It sucks. (*mildly vulgar*)
It reeks. (*informal*)
My kid could do that.
It's awful.
It's terrible.
It's ugly.
It's hideous.
It's dreadful.
It's hell on earth. (*informal*)
I don't get it.
Don't quit your day job.

35 Expressing refusal

No.

Nope. (*informal*)

No way.

No way, Jose. (*informal*)

No can do. (*informal*)

No, sir.

No sirree. (*folksy*)

No sirree, Bob. (*folksy*)

Sorry.

Nothing doing.

You're out of luck.

In a pig's eye. (*idiomatic*)

When pigs fly. (*idiomatic*)

When hell freezes over. (*informal*)

There isn't a snowball's chance in hell. (*informal*)

Not a chance.

No chance.

Not if I can help it.

Not likely.

Not bloody likely. (*mildly vulgar*)

Absolutely not!

It will be a cold day in hell before I do that. (*informal*)

Only in your dreams.

Dream on.

Save your breath.

Save it.

You're barking up the wrong tree. (*idiomatic*)

Over my dead body. (*idiomatic*)

Forget it.

If you think that, you've got another think coming.

Not in a million years.

Not for a million dollars.

You couldn't pay me to do it.
Not in your wildest dreams.
You wish.
I'll be damned first. (*mildly vulgar*)
I'll be damned if I do. (*mildly vulgar*)
Damned if I will. (*mildly vulgar*)
Like hell. (*mildly vulgar*)
I'll see you in hell first. (*mildly vulgar*)
You're S.O.L. (*vulgar*)
> S.O.L. = *shit out of luck*

36 Stating that someone is wrong

What are you talking about?
You don't know what you're talking about.
You don't have a leg to stand on.
You haven't got a leg to stand on.
You don't know the first thing about it.
You're really stretching the truth.
You're way off base.
You can lay that notion to rest.

37 Arguing about the facts

You've got it all wrong.
You've got the facts wrong.
You've got your facts wrong.
You haven't got the facts.
You haven't got the facts right.
I don't think you've got your facts straight.
Don't speak until you've got your facts straight.
Next time get the facts straight. (*informal*)
Next time get the facts first. (*informal*)
Don't jump to conclusions.

CONVERSATIONAL ENCOUNTERS

FOCUSING ATTENTION

38 **Getting someone's attention**

Pardon me. (*formal*)

Excuse me.

Hey! (*informal*)

Hey, you! (*informal*)

Yo! (*slang*)

39 **Getting someone to listen to you**

Look here. (*informal*)

Listen here. (*informal*)

Listen up. (*informal*)

Get a load of this. (*informal*)

Now hear this! (*informal*)

Hear me out.

Are you ready for this? (*informal*)

Listen. (*informal*)

Are you listening to me?

Are you paying attention?

I'm talking to you.

Do you hear me?

Do I have your ear? (*idiomatic*)

Can I bend your ear a minute? (*idiomatic*)

Am I making myself heard?

40 **Directing attention to an object**

Look at this.

Take a look at this.

Get a load of this.

Take a gander at that. (*informal*)

    a gander = a look

Feast your eyes on this.

Look what we have here.

Lookie here. (*informal*)

Lookit. (*slang*)

Look here.

Can you eyeball this (for a minute)? (*slang*)

    to eyeball = to look at

Can you believe your eyes?

I don't believe my eyes.

Do my eyes deceive me?

That's a sight for sore eyes.

41   Confirming that you are paying attention

I hear you.

I heard you.

I'm listening.

I'm still here.

I'm all ears.

LAUNCHING THE CONVERSATION

42   Starting an informal conversation

Guess what?

Have you heard the latest?

Have you heard?

Did you hear what happened?

Did you hear the news?

Did you get the scoop? (*informal*)

    the scoop = the most recent news

You'll never guess what I heard.

Guess what I just found out.

You won't believe this.

You won't believe what Bill just told me.

Get a load of this. (*informal*)

    a load = a sampling

Get this. (*informal*)

Dig this. (*slang*)

    to dig = to understand

43   Inviting someone to talk

You got a minute?

Got a minute?

I need to talk.

Can we talk?

Can I talk to you?

May I have a word with you? (*formal*)

Let's talk.

Let's chew the fat. (*slang*)

Let's shoot the breeze. (*slang*)

44   Coming to the point of the matter

May I be frank?

Let me be perfectly clear.

Make no bones about it. (*idiomatic*)

    = Do not make any bones of contention about this

Read my lips. (*informal*)

    = Pay close attention to what I am saying.

(To make a) long story short. (*cliché*)

Let's call a spade a spade. (*cliché*)

Let me spell it out for you.

Here's the bottom line.

    the bottom line = the summation; the final and major
    point

45 Requesting that the speaker get to the point

What's your point?

What's the point?

What's the upshot?

> *the upshot = the result*

What's the bottom line?

> *the bottom line = the summation; the final and major point*

What are you trying to say?

What are you trying to tell me?

Get to the point.

Get to the heart of the matter.

Cut to the chase. (*idiomatic*)

> *= Switch to the focal point of something.*

46 Various conversational phrases

If I may.

> *= If I may interrupt.; If I may add some information.*

Pardon my French.

> *= Pardon my use of vulgar words.*

No pun intended.

> *= I intended to make no joke or play on words.*

If you know what I mean.

> *= I assume you understand what I mean.*

Know what I mean? (*informal*)

> *= Do you understand what I am saying?*

You know what I'm saying?

> *= Do you understand what I am saying?*

You know?

> *= Do you understand what I am saying?*

Right?

> *= Is that not so?*

OK?

> *= Is that not so?*

47   Encouraging someone to speak plainly

Enough already. (*informal*)

Out with it! (*informal*)

> = *Say it!; Speak out!*

Don't mince words.

> *to mince = to cut up or disguise*

Spare (me) nothing.

Lay it on the line. (*informal*)

Tell it to me like a man. (*informal*)

Give it to me straight. (*informal*)

> *straight = unadorned*

Give it to me in plain English.

> *plain English = simple and direct terms*

Don't beat around the bush. (*idiomatic*)

Stop beating around the bush. (*idiomatic*)

Stop circumventing the issue.

Put your cards on the table. (*idiomatic*)

Stop speaking in circles.

What does that mean in English? (*informal*)

Cut the crap. (*mildly vulgar*)

> *crap = dung = needless talk*

48   Noting digressions in a conversation

That's beside the point.

That's beside the question.

That's not at issue.

That's not the issue.

That's irrelevant.

That has nothing to do with it.

That has nothing to do with what I'm talking about.

That's another story.

That's a whole 'nother story. (*folksy*)

That's a different ball of wax. (*idiomatic*)

> *ball of wax = thing; matter*

That's a different kettle of fish. (*idiomatic*)

> *kettle of fish = thing; matter*

That's another can of worms. (*idiomatic*)

> *can of worms = set of problems*

That's a horse of a different color. (*idiomatic*)

> *a horse of a different color = a different kind of problem altogether*

You're off on a tangent.

You're getting off the subject.

As you were saying . . .

Getting back to the point . . .

But I digress. (*formal*)

49   Repeating what you have said

Let me repeat myself.

Allow me to repeat myself. (*formal*)

As I've said . . .

As I am fond of saying . . .

To reiterate . . .

To repeat . . .

How many times do I have to tell you?

If I've told you once, I've told you a thousand times. (*cliché*)

If I've said it once, I've said it a million times. (*cliché*)

50   When someone is being repetitious

So you said.

Stop beating a dead horse.

> *beating a dead horse = continuing to argue a point that has been won*

Stop harping on that subject.

> *harping on = dwelling on; talking about*

You sound like a broken record. (*idiomatic*)

> *broken record = a grooved LP album with a scratch that makes the same track repeat endlessly*

Must you belabor the point?

All right, already.

We get the point, already.

We heard you, already.

51   Agreeing with a speaker

So it seems.

So it would seem.

Or so it would appear.

As it were.

So to speak.

In a manner of speaking.

52   Answers to "How did you find out?"

I heard it through the grapevine.

> *the grapevine = a chain of rumors*

I heard it on the grapevine.

A little bird told me. (*cliché*)

I have my sources.

I got it straight from the horse's mouth. (*idiomatic*)

> *from the horse's mouth = from the source*

It's common knowledge.

We live in a fishbowl. (*informal*)

> *= We are completely on display.; We are openly visible to everyone.*

Word travels fast. (*cliché*)

News travels fast. (*cliché*)

Bad news travels fast. (*cliché*)

None of your business. (*informal*)

Just never (you) mind.

We have our ways (of finding these things out). (*jocular*)

I plead the fifth. (*informal*)

> *the fifth = the Fifth Amendment to the U.S. Constitution, which protects against self-incrimination*

I'm not one to kiss and tell. (*cliché*)

> *to kiss and tell = to do something secret and tell everyone about it*

MAKING FRIENDS

53   **Expressing friendship**

We're very close.

We're the closest of friends.

We're the best of friends.

We're best friends.

We're pretty tight.

Their bosom buddies.

She's my best friend.

She's my closest friend.

She's a dear friend.

She's like a sister to me.

He's like the brother I never had.

We're like brothers.

54   **Commenting on the uniqueness of someone**

He's one of a kind.

Sue's one of a kind.

What a character!

They don't make them like him anymore. (*cliché*)

After they made him, they broke the mold. (*cliché*)

55   **Commenting on personal similarities**

We're two of a kind.

They're two of a kind.

We're cut from the same cloth.

We're made from the same mold.

We're birds of a feather. (*cliché*)

We're like two peas in a pod.

56   Expressions used to make friends at a bar or café
May I join you?
Is this stool taken?
Is this seat taken?
Do you care if I join you?
Care if I join you?
Do you mind if I join you?
Mind if I join you?
Care to join us?
Can I buy you a drink?
Could I buy you a drink?
Could I get you something to drink?
What are you drinking?
Do you know who does this song?
>   *does = sings*

Would you like to play darts?
Let's play pool.
>   *pool = billiards*

57   Inviting someone to dance
Care to dance?
Would you like to dance?
You want to dance? (*informal*)
Could I have the next dance?
May I have the next dance? (*formal*)

58   Approaching the opposite sex
That's a pretty outfit. (*male to female*)
That's a pretty dress. (*male to female*)
What's your sign?
>   *sign = sign of the zodiac*

What's shaking? (*slang*)
>   *shaking = happening*

Don't I know you from somewhere?

Didn't we go to high school together?

Haven't I seen you here before?

Do you come here often?

What's a nice girl like you doing in a place like this?
  (*male to female, cliché*)

Do you have a smoke?

  a smoke = a cigarette

Do you have a light?

  a light = a match or cigarette lighter

Do you have a cigarette?

Do you have change for the cigarette machine?

Are you going my way?

Going my way? (*cliché*)

Could I give you a lift?

  a lift = a ride

Need a lift?

Where have you been keeping yourself?

Where have you been all my life? (*cliché*)

59   Bringing a conversation to an end

Let's call it a day.

Let's call it a night.

Let's call it quits.

  = Let's quit (and leave).

Let's get out of here.

Let's get going.

Let's go.

We should be on our way.

Let's bid our farewell. (*formal*)

Let's say our good-byes. (*formal*)

COMPLEX MATTERS

60 **Expressing support for someone**

I'll stand by you.

I'm standing behind you.

I am 100% behind you.

I'm with you.

I'm on your side.

You've got my support.

You've got my backing.

You've got my vote.

You can count on me.

You can lean on me.

You can trust me.

You can put your trust in me.

You can put your faith in me.

61 **Offering help to someone**

If there's anything I can do to help, please let me know.

Let me know if there's anything I can do.

I'm here if you need me.

I'm here for you.

If you need me, call.

I'll always be there for you.

I'll go to bat for you.

　　to go to bat for you = to support you

I'll take the rap. (*slang*)

　　the rap = the blame

62 **Expressing trust in someone**

I have faith in you.

I have the utmost faith in you.

I have complete faith in you.

I trust you completely.

I trust you implicitly.

I have faith in you.

I have confidence in you.

63 Expressing encouragement

Go on; you can do it!

Just one more.

Just a little harder.

Stick with it.

Stay at it.

Go for it.

Give it a try.

Give it a shot.

> *a shot = a try*

Give it your best shot.

Give it your best.

Give it the old college try. (*cliché*)

> *the old college try = a noble effort*

Keep at it.

Keep your nose to the grindstone. (*idiomatic*)

> *= Keep bent over your work. = Keep working hard.*

Hang in there. (*informal*)

Hang tough. (*slang*)

Stick it out. (*informal*)

64 Encouraging someone to try something

Have a go at it.

> *a go = a try*

Take a shot at it. (*informal*)

> *a shot = a try*

Take a stab at it. (*informal*)

> *a stab = a try*

Take a crack at it. (*informal*)

> a crack = a try

Have a crack at it.

Take a whack at it. (*informal*)

> a whack = a try

Come on. (*informal*)

It won't hurt you to try it.

Everybody's doing it.

Everyone else is doing it.

It's all the rage.

> the rage = the current fad

Try your luck.

See what you can do.

Nothing ventured, nothing gained. (*cliché*)

Go on.

Get going.

Get going already.

Get moving.

No pain, no gain. (*cliché*)

Get a move on. (*informal*)

Get cracking. (*slang*)

Get on the stick. (*slang*)

Get the lead out. (*slang*)

Get off your ass. (*mildly vulgar*)

65 Encouraging someone to stop stalling and do something

Let's see some action. (*informal*)

It's now or never.

Take no prisoners! (*informal*)

Fish or cut bait! (*idiomatic*)

Knock yourself out. (*idiomatic*)

> = Try really hard.; Work as hard as you can.

Go for broke. (*informal*)

> = *Risk everything.*

I expect to see some results soon.

Are you just going to stand there all day?

Are you just going to sit there?

Aren't you going to do anything?

Are you just going to sit there like a bump on a log? (*informal*)

> *a bump on a log = a motionless object*

You're letting the world pass you by.

66   Expressing dissatisfaction with someone's efforts

That won't do.

That won't do it.

That doesn't cut it. (*idiomatic*)

> *to cut it = to do what is needed*

That doesn't cut the mustard. (*idiomatic*)

> *to cut the mustard = to measure up to expectations*

That doesn't make the grade.

> *to make the grade = to qualify*

Is that it?

It's not up to snuff.

Is that all?

You call that finished?

Once more with feeling. (*cliché*)

67   Asking someone to wait

Wait.

Wait a moment.

Wait a minute.

Wait a sec(ond).

Wait one moment.

Wait one minute.

Wait one sec(ond).

Wait it out.

Wait your turn.

Just a moment.

Just a minute.

Just a sec(ond).

Just one moment.

Just one minute.

Just one sec(ond).

Hold your horses. (*idiomatic*)

  = *Wait a bit.*

Hold your pants on. (*informal*)

  = *Wait a bit.*

Keep your pants on. (*informal*)

Keep your shirt on. (*informal*)

  = *Wait a bit.*

68   Encouraging someone to be patient and take things slowly

Take things as they come.

Take it as it comes.

Take it one day at a time.

Take things one day at a time.

Take one day at a time.

Time will tell. (*cliché*)

  = *We will know more in time.*

Rome wasn't built in a day. (*cliché*)

  = *Big projects require a lot of time.*

A watched pot never boils. (*cliché*)

  = *Paying constant attention to something you are waiting for will make the wait seem endless.*

Good things come to **him** who waits. (*cliché*)

One step at at time.

One day at a time.

Good things come to those who wait. (*cliché*)

Patience is a virtue. (*cliché*)

In good time.

All in good time.

Everything in its time.

There's a time for everything.

It will work out in the end.

Everything will come together.

Everything will fall together.

Everything will fall into place.

In the long run, everything will be OK. (*informal*)

In the long haul, it will all work out.

Everything will work itself out.

I am confident it will all work out.

It ain't over till it's over. (*informal*)

It ain't over till the fat lady sings. (*cliché*)

> = *The opera is not over until the overweight opera singer has done her solo.* = *The event will not conclude until everything that was planned to happen has happened.*

69   Encouraging someone to be prudent — clichés

Don't jump the gun.

> *to jump the gun* = *to start a race before the starting gun is fired* = *to do something too early*

Don't go off half-cocked.

> *half-cocked* = *ill-prepared*

Don't go chomping at the bit.

> *chomp* = *to bite (as with an eager horse)*

Don't put the cart before the horse.

Don't count your chickens before they hatch.

> = *Don't base your plans on something that hasn't developed yet.*

Don't cross that bridge till you come to it.

> = *We will deal with that when the time comes.*

We'll cross that bridge when we come to it.

Don't get ahead of yourself.

70 Giving advice to someone whose life is too busy

You can't please everybody. (*cliché*)

You can't be all things to all people. (*cliché*)

You've got your fingers in too many pies. (*idiomatic*)

You've got your irons in too many fires. (*idiomatic*)

You're burning the candle at both ends. (*cliché*)

You're taking too many things on.

You're taking on too much.

You're doing too much.

You're trying to do too much.

You're overcommitted.

You're overdoing it.

You're carrying the world on your shoulders.

You need to set your priorities.

71 Giving instructions to someone you've lent something to

Take care of it.

Take good care of it.

I'm trusting you to take good care of it.

Keep an eye on it.

Guard it with your life.

Don't let it out of your sight.

I want this back.

I want it back in one piece.

> *in one piece = unbroken; unharmed*

Bring it back in one piece.

72 Introducing a secret

Just between you and me . . .

Just between you, me, and the lamppost . . .

This is between you, me, and the bedpost.
This is between you, me, and the four walls.
I'm telling you this in confidence.
I'm telling you this in strict confidence.
I'm telling you this in strictest confidence.
Can you keep a secret?
Don't repeat this, but . . .
Don't let this get around, but . . .
Could you keep a secret?
Confidentially . . .

73 **Instructions about keeping a secret**
Better keep quiet about it.
Better keep still about it.
Keep it to yourself.
Don't breathe a word of this to anyone.
Don't breathe a word of it.
Don't let it out of this room.
> *it = the secret*

Don't let this go any further.
Don't tell a soul.
> *a soul = a person*

Mum's the word.
> *mum = a word referring to a closed mouth*

It's on the QT. (*slang*)
> *QT = quiet*

Play dumb.
This is top secret.
This is for your eyes only.
This is for your ears only.
Don't say I told you.
Don't say who told you.
This is off the record.
> *off the record = not to be reported or quoted*

This is not for the record.
This is not to be quoted.
This is not for public knowledge.
This is not public knowledge.
This is not for publication.

74 Promising to keep a secret

I won't tell a soul.

> *a soul = a person*

My lips are sealed. (*cliché*)

It won't leave this room.

Wild horses couldn't drag it out of me. (*cliché*)

I'll take it to my grave.

> = *I'll die without telling the secret to anyone.*

75 Forgetfulness

Where was I?

> = *What was I saying?*

What was I saying?

What were we talking about?

I don't remember.

I have a mind like a sieve.

> *a sieve = a strainer or colander*

I'm a little absentminded.

> *absentminded = forgetful*

I'd lose my head if it weren't attached. (*informal*)

I've lost my train of thought.

> *train of thought = sequence of thoughts*

It's at the tip of my tongue.

> = *It is about ready to be said.*

It's on the tip of my tongue.

It's slipped my mind.

The thought escapes me.

It's left my head.

What was your name again?

What did you just say?

It went in one ear and out the other. (*cliché*)

Are we supposed to be someplace right now?

76 When you are in trouble

I'm in trouble.

I'm in big trouble.

I'm in deep trouble.

I'm in deep.

I'm in over my head.

I'm in way over my head.

I'm behind the eight ball. (*idiomatic*)

   = *I'm in trouble with someone.*

My ass is in a sling. (*mildly vulgar*)

   in a sling = injured

My ass is on the line. (*mildly vulgar*)

   on the line = at risk

My neck is on the line.

My job is on the line.

My reputation is on the line.

My reputation is at stake.

   at stake = at risk

77 When someone is in trouble

Your goose is cooked. (*idiomatic*)

   = *You are in trouble.*

You've really screwed up. (*informal*)

You've done it now.

Now you've done it.

You've really done it this time.

You're in for it.

You're gonna get it. (*informal*)

How could you do something so stupid?

What kind of mess did you get yourself into?

That's another fine mess you've gotten us into. (*informal*)

How are you going to dig yourself out of this one?

How are you going to get out of this one?

You've made your bed; now lie in it.

> = *You have created this situation, so you must endure it.*

You're up the creek without a paddle. (*informal*)

You're up a creek. (*informal*)

You're up the creek. (*informal*)

78   When you are out of money

I'm broke.

> *broke = without any money*

I'm dead broke.

I'm flat broke.

I'm flatter than a pancake. (*informal*)

> *flatter than a pancake = as flat broke as is possible*

I don't have a dollar to my name.

> *to my name = in my ownership*

I don't have a penny to my name.

I don't have a cent to my name.

I don't have a red cent. (*informal*)

> *red cent = a copper penny*

I'm busted. (*slang*)

> *busted = without any money*

I'm as poor as a church mouse. (*idiomatic*)

My pockets are empty.

I have empty pockets.

All I have is the shirt on my back.

> *the shirt on my back = the clothes that you see me in*

I've got nothing but the shirt on my back.

All I have is my good name.

> *my good name = my reputation*

I don't know where my next meal is coming from.
My savings are wiped out.
I've lost everything.
I'm bankrupt.

79   When someone is in debt

I'm in the red.

> *red = red ink = indebtedness*

She's in over her head (in debt). (*idiomatic*)
I'm up to my ears in debt. (*idiomatic*)
Bill's writing rubber checks.

> *a rubber check = a bad check (that bounces back from the bank because there is no money to pay it)*

I'm borrowing from Peter to pay Paul. (*idiomatic*)
I'm robbing Peter to pay Paul. (*idiomatic*)

80   Expressing stress or anxiety

I'm going nuts. (*slang*)

> *nuts = crazy*

I'm going crazy.
I'm losing my mind.
I'm losing my marbles. (*informal*)

> *losing my marbles = losing my intellect*

I'm freaking out. (*slang*)
I'm spazzing out. (*slang*)
I'm mad at the world.
I need a break.
I need some sleep.
I'm going to explode.
My head is going to explode.
Everything is getting on my nerves.
I can't take it anymore.
I can't take another problem.
I can't deal with this anymore.

I'm on pins and needles. (*idiomatic*)

> *on pins and needles = in anxious anticipation*

I'm on tenterhooks.

> *tenterhooks = a type of sharp nail used for fastening fabric*

I'm a bundle of nerves.

I've got butterflies in my stomach. (*idiomatic*)

> *= My stomach is feeling like it is fluttering.*

I'm coming apart at the seams.

I'm falling apart at the seams.

81   When you are overworked and doing too much

I'm burning the candle at both ends. (*cliché*)

I scarcely have time to breathe.

I have no time to call my own.

82   When someone is anxious and under stress

Calm down.

Simmer down.

Control yourself. (*informal*)

Don't go into hysterics.

Don't be such a worrywart.

> *a worrywart = a person who worries a lot*

Don't worry yourself sick.

Don't lose sleep over it.

Don't let it get to you.

Don't trouble yourself.

You'll send yourself to an early grave.

> *an early grave = an early death*

**83   Encouraging someone not to be offended —
       informal**

Don't get all bent out of shape!

Don't get your nose out of joint!

Don't be so sensitive!

Learn to roll with the punches.

I didn't mean any harm.

84 Encouraging someone not to be excited

Pull yourself together.

Don't get excited.

Don't get all excited.

Don't get all worked up.

Don't blow your stack. (*slang*)

> to blow your stack = to lose your temper; to go crazy

Don't lose your cool. (*slang*)

Don't blow your cool. (*slang*)

Don't blow a gasket. (*slang*)

Don't go into hysterics.

Don't go into hysterics on me.

Don't fly off the handle.

Don't pop your cork. (*slang*)

> to pop your cork = to go crazy

Don't work yourself into a tizzy. (*informal*)

> a tizzy = a dizzy, confused state

Don't run around like a chicken with its head cut off. (*informal*)

Restrain yourself.

Would you restrain yourself?

Get a grip (on yourself). (*informal*)

Would you get a grip? (*informal*)

85 Encouraging someone to relax

Mellow out. (*slang*)

> = Adopt a calm attitude.

Chill out. (*slang*)

Chill. (*slang*)

Keep cool. (*slang*)

Cool it. (*slang*)

Cool your jets. (*slang*)

Cool off. (*informal*)

Cool down. (*informal*)

Slow down.

Simmer down.

Calm down.

Be calm.

Calm yourself.

Relax.

Deal with it. (*informal*)

Hold your horses. (*cliché*)

Keep your shirt on. (*informal*)

Keep your pants on. (*informal*)

Take a deep breath.

Take it easy.

Take it slow.

Take a tranquilizer! (*informal*)

Take a pill! (*informal*)

**86   Encouraging someone to be less aggressive —
informal**

Don't have a cow!

Don't have a conniption fit.

Don't throw a fit.

Don't have a fit.

Give it a break.

Give it a rest.

You got ants in your pants?

87   When someone is cold and unfeeling — informal

You're as cold as ice.

You're a cold fish.

You're cold-blooded.

You've got a heart of stone.

You've got no heart.

You're heartless.

You're thick-skinned.

Have you no qualms?

Have you no scruples?

Have you no conscience?

Have you no thought for anyone but yourself?

Think before you speak.

Think before you act.

Try putting yourself in my shoes.

    = *Think what it is like to be in my situation.*

88   **What to say to a smoker**

This is a nonsmoking area.

This is a nonsmoking building.

You'll have to step outside.

Please observe the no smoking signs. (*formal*)

Can you put that out?

Please put that out.

I'm sorry, you'll have to put that out.

I'm sorry, the smoke is bothering me.

Have you ever thought of quitting?

It's your funeral. (*informal*)

You smoke like a chimney. (*informal*)

89   **A smoker's response to a nonsmoker's complaint**

Mind your own business.

Go to a nonsmoking area.

I can't quit.

I tried quitting.

I have no intention of quitting.

Sorry.

90   Questions a smoker might ask

Got a match?

You got a lighter?

Can I bum a light?

>   *to bum = to beg*

Can I bum a cigarette off you?

Can I have a drag?

>   *a drag = a puff of smoke*

Where is the smoking room?

Where can you smoke around here?

Do you mind if I smoke?

DISPUTES

91   Criticism of someone with whom you disagree

You're clueless. (*informal*)

You're without a clue. (*informal*)

You wouldn't know the truth if it jumped up and bit you
on the nose. (*jocular*)

She doesn't know nothing. (*informal*)

You don't know beans. (*informal*)

You don't know up from down. (*informal*)

You don't know which end is up. (*informal*)

You don't know your ass from your elbow. (*vulgar*)

You don't know your ass from a hole in the ground.
(*vulgar*)

You don't know quality from a hole in the ground.
(*informal*)

>   *quality ≈ art, value, truth, engines, etc.*

Don't you know anything?

How can you be so stupid? (*informal*)

Get your head out of the sand. (*idiomatic*)

That ain't the way I heard it. (*folksy*)

That's not what I heard.

Let me set you straight.

92   Calling someone crazy

You're off your rocker. (*informal*)

You're out of your mind. (*informal*)

He's two bricks shy of a load. (*slang*)

You're out of your tree. (*slang*)

You're out of your head. (*informal*)

She's out of her skull. (*informal*)

You've lost your marbles. (*informal*)

You're crazy. (*informal*)

You're nuts. (*informal*)

They can't be serious.

You're a few cards shy of a full deck. (*idiomatic*)

You're a few cards short of a deck. (*idiomatic*)

You aren't playing with a full deck. (*idiomatic*)

You're one sandwich short of a picnic. (*idiomatic*)

Your front porch light is out.

You've gone over the edge.

You've gone off the deep end.

You're nutty as a fruitcake. (*cliché*)

93   Questioning someone's sanity

Are you crazy?

Is he nuts? (*slang*)

    nuts = crazy

Are you psychotic, or what?

Are you out of your mind?

Are you out of your head?

Are you out of your gourd? (*informal*)

    gourd = head

Are you out of your skull? (*informal*)

Are you out of your tree? (*slang*)

Are you out of it?

Have you gone crazy?

Have you gone insane?

Have you gone mad?

Have you gone stark raving mad?

Have you gone loco? (*informal*)

>   *loco (Spanish)* = crazy

Have you gone plumb loco? (*informal*)

>   *plumb loco = completely crazy*

Have you lost your mind?

Have you lost your senses?

Have you lost your marbles?

Have you wigged out? (*slang*)

Have you completely flipped out? (*slang*)

Have you flipped your lid? (*slang*)

Have you completely lost it? (*informal*)

Have you completely lost touch with reality?

Have you taken leave of your senses?

Do you have a screw loose? (*slang*)

What planet are you from?

Do you have rocks in your head? (*informal*)

Do you have bats in your belfry? (*slang*)

Are there bats in your belfry? (*slang*)

Are you playing with a full deck? (*slang*)

94 Asking about the alertness of someone

Hello? (*informal*)

What are you thinking?

What's your deal? (*informal*)

What's your problem? (*informal*)

What ((kind of) drugs) are you on? (*informal*)

What have you been smoking? (*informal*)

Where's your head? (*informal*)

What's with you? (*informal*)

Are you serious?

What planet are you on? (*informal*)

Earth to Bill. (*informal*)

95 **Encouraging someone to be more sensible**

Get a life! (*informal*)

Get real!

Snap out of it.

Come back to earth. (*informal*)

96 **Asking in disbelief or disagreement**

Truly?

Really?

For real? (*informal*)

No kidding?

No fooling? (*informal*)

No lie? (*informal*)

No way! (*informal*)

Are you serious?

Are you for real? (*informal*)

Are you pulling my leg?

Are you bullshitting me? (*mildly vulgar*)

You're not making this up, are you?

You're making this up, aren't you?

You're not trying to pull one over on me, are you?

97 **When someone says something outrageous**

Unbelievable!

Get out of town!

You're kidding!

You've got to be kidding!

You've got to be kidding me!

Stop it! (*informal*)

Come on! (*informal*)

Get out of here! (*informal*)

I can't believe it!

Do you expect me to believe that?

That blows my mind. (*informal*)

DISCUSSION AND RESOLUTION

98   Asking for an explanation

What do you mean?

What are you saying?

What are you trying to get at?

What are you getting at?

Do you mean to tell me?

What's the bottom line?

This all boils down to what? (*idiomatic*)

How so?

So what's the upshot?

What's the point?

99   Encouraging an explanation

I didn't get that.

I didn't hear you.

Cut to the chase. (*idiomatic*)

100   When you do not understand someone

I don't see what you're getting at.

I don't get it.

I don't follow you.

I don't follow.

I'm not sure I follow.

I'm not sure I get your point.

I'm not sure I know what you mean.

101 When someone does not understand you

That's not what I meant.

That's not what I said.

I didn't mean that.

I didn't say that.

I said no such thing.

I didn't mean to give you that impression.

I didn't mean to imply that.

102 Criticizing someone's misunderstanding

Listen to me.

Open your ears. (*informal*)

Get the wax out of your ears. (*informal*)

You're not listening to what I'm saying.

You're only hearing what you want to hear.

You're missing the point.

That's not my point.

That's not the point I'm trying to make.

You've got it wrong.

You've got it all wrong.

You've got me wrong.

You've twisted my words.

You're putting words in my mouth.

You're quoting me out of context.

You're taking it out of context.

You're blowing it out of proportion.

You're blowing this all out of proportion.

103 Attempting to put an end to a misunderstanding

Let me rephrase that.

Let me clarify that.

Allow me to clarify.

Let me make myself clear.

Let me make myself perfectly clear.

104   Encouraging someone to believe you

Honest.

Honestly.

Truly.

True.

That's the truth.

That's the honest truth.

That's the honest-to-goodness truth.

Honest to goodness.

That's the truth, the whole truth, and nothing but the truth.

Cross my heart and hope to die. (*juvenile*)

Would I lie?

Would I lie to you?

Why would I lie?

I swear.

I swear to you.

I swear on a stack of Bibles. (*mild oath*)

I swear on my mother's grave. (*informal*)

I swear to God. (*mild oath*)

May God strike me down if I am not telling you the truth. (*mild oath*)

That's the gospel truth. (*informal*)

105   Asking to be trusted

Take my word for it.

You have my word.

You have my word on this.

I give you my word.

I give you my word of honor.

On my honor.

Scout's honor. (*juvenile*)

You can count on it.

You can bank on it.

You can take it to the bank.

You better believe it.

You had better believe it.

Believe you me.

Trust me.

Don't be such a doubting Thomas.

106 **Stating that something is settled**

It's cinched.

It's locked up.

It's sewn up.

It's a sure thing.

It's for sure.

It's certain.

It's in the bag.

It's a done deal.

It's as good as done.

Nothing can go wrong.

What can go wrong?

All's well that ends well. (*cliché*)

That's that.

What's to go wrong?

It's going to happen.

There's no doubt in my mind.

There's not a doubt in my mind.

107 **Claiming that something is easy to understand**

It's as plain as day.

It's as clear as day.

It's as plain as the nose on your face. (*jocular*)

Do I need to paint you a picture? (*informal*)

Must I paint you a picture? (*informal*)

That goes without saying.

Any fool can see it. (*informal*)

108 Showing disbelief

I find that hard to believe.

Unbelievable.

I find that hard to swallow.

I'll take that with a grain of salt. (*cliché*)

I remain skeptical.

I'll believe it when I see it.

You can't fool me.

You can't pull the wool over my eyes.

I wasn't born yesterday.

109 Expressing ignorance

Dunno. (*informal*)

I don't know.

I don't know and I don't care.

I don't have a clue.

I haven't a clue.

I'm clueless.

I don't have the faintest idea.

I haven't the faintest idea.

I haven't the vaguest notion.

I don't have the foggiest notion.

Haven't the foggiest.

Beats me. (*informal*)

Beats the heck out of me. (*informal*)

Beats the hell out of me. (*mildly vulgar*)

Got me beat. (*informal*)

You got me (there).

Got me stumped. (*informal*)

Got me.

How would I know?

How should I know?

How the hell should I know? (*mildly vulgar*)

Like I would know. (*informal*)
Like I would know? (*informal*)
I give up. (*informal*)
Search me. (*informal*)
Who knows?
Lord knows. (*mild oath*)
God only knows. (*mild oath*)

110   Expressing reluctance
I'm afraid not.
'Fraid not.
I'm afraid so.
'Fraid so.
If I must. (*formal*)
Well, if I have to.
Well, if you insist.
Well, if you really think so.
Well, if you really want me to.
I guess I have no choice in the matter.
It doesn't sound like I have a choice.
We've got no choice.
We have no alternative.
There's no alternative.
I'd rather not.
I'd rather die.
I'd sooner die.
Never in a thousand years.
Not in a million years.
Over my dead body. (*informal*)

111   Making the best of a bad situation
That's life.
That's the way life is.
That's how it goes.

That's the way it goes.

That's the way the ball bounces. (*cliché*)

That's the way the cookie crumbles. (*cliché*)

Things could be worse.

It's not as bad as all that.

Look on the bright(er) side. (*cliché*)

Make the best of it.

Half a loaf is better than none. (*cliché*)

It's always darkest before dawn. (*cliché*)

Every cloud has a silver lining. (*cliché*)

When life hands you lemons, make lemonade. (*cliché*)

It's the best we can do under the circumstances.

I wish we could do more.

You did the best you could.

You did the best that could be expected.

You get an A for effort.

The important thing is that you tried.

Winning isn't everything. (*cliché*)

You can't win them all. (*cliché*)

It's not whether you win or lose, it's how you play the game. (*cliché*)

You made a noble effort.

Truth is stranger than fiction. (*cliché*)

It was just one of those things. (*cliché*)

(Don't ask why;) it just is.

Why ask why? (*informal*)

Who am I to question?

It's for the best. (*cliché*)

It's all for the best. (*cliché*)

When God closes a door, He opens a window. (*cliché*)

Don't let it get you down.

Keep your chin up! (*cliché*)

Chin up!

Cheer up!

Keep a stiff upper lip. (*cliché*)

Grin and bear it. (*cliché*)

Grit your teeth. (*cliché*)

Take it in stride. (*cliché*)

Roll with the punches. (*cliché*)

Accept your fate.

You've made your bed; now lie in it. (*cliché*)

If at first you don't succeed, try, try again. (*cliché*)

The important thing is to learn from your mistakes.

The third time's the charm. (*cliché*)

I'm between a rock and a hard place. (*cliché*)

I'm between the devil and the deep blue sea. (*cliché*)

I'm damned if I do and damned if I don't. (*mildly vulgar*)

You're damned if you do and damned if you don't.
(*mildly vulgar*)

112   Blaming something on fate or destiny

It was destiny.

It was destined to happen.

It's your fate.

It was fated to happen.

It's fate.

It's in the cards.

It's in the stars.

It's the cruel hand of fate.

That's karma.

It's God's will.

It's all in God's plan.

It was meant to be.

Que sera, sera. (*Spanish*)
   = *Whatever will be, will be.*

What will be, will be.

Whatever will be, will be.

Don't fight it.

You can't fight it.

You can't fight City Hall.

There's nothing you can do about it.

You have to play the hand life deals you.

You've got to play the hand you're dealt.

113 Knowing something after the fact

I should have known.

I should have known better.

If I (only) knew then what I know now . . .

If I (just) knew then what I know now . . .

If I'd known then what I know now . . .

If only I could turn back the hands of time.

If I could only turn back the clock.

It's easy to be wise after the event.

That's easy to say in hindsight.

Hindsight is 20/20.

20/20 = good vision in each eye at twenty feet

20/20 hindsight.

114 Expressing indifference

I don't care.

I couldn't care less.

I could care less. (*informal*)

I don't give a damn. (*mildly vulgar*)

Like I give a damn. (*mildly vulgar*)

It doesn't matter to me.

Really doesn't matter to me.

Makes no difference to me.

Makes me no difference. (*informal*)

Makes me no nevermind. (*folksy*)

Makes no nevermind to me. (*folksy*)

Either way.

Whichever.

Whatever.

Six of one, half (a) dozen of the other. (*informal*)

Up to you.

Whatever you prefer.

It's not important.

I guess so.

I guess.

POLITE ENCOUNTERS

PREFACES

115 **A preface to asking a question**

Excuse me . . .

Pardon me . . .

Excuse me for asking . . .

If you don't mind my asking . . .

It's none of my business, but . . .

116 **A preface to making a statement — formal**

If I may say so . . .

If I may be so bold . . .

If it's okay with you . . .

If it pleases you . . .

Please be advised that . . .

For your information . . .

It is a pleasure to inform you that . . .

We regret to inform you that . . .

As you are aware . . .

As you are no doubt aware . . .

As you know . . .

As you might know . . .

As you may already know . . .

117 **A preface to making a statement — informal**

(To make a) long story short . . .

What I would like to say is . . .

But I just wanted to say . . .

By the way . . .

If you ask me . . .

Not that it's any of my business . . .

118   A preface to making a statement — very polite

As you requested . . .

For your convenience . . .

We apologize for the inconvenience . . .

With your safety in mind . . .

With your comfort in mind . . .

COMMUNICATION BARRIERS

119   Asking if someone speaks a particular language

Do you speak French?

> *French ≈ Spanish, German, Russian, Italian, etc.*

Do you know any French?

Do you speak any French?

120   When you do not speak a particular language

I'm sorry. I don't understand.

I'm sorry. I don't speak French.

> *French ≈ Spanish, German, Russian, Italian, etc.*

I'm sorry. My French isn't very good.

I only speak a little French.

121   When you do not understand what was said

Pardon me?

Excuse me?

Again(, please).

I'm sorry?

I'm sorry. I missed that.

> *missed that = failed to hear what was said*

I didn't quite get that.

> *to get that = to hear or understand what was said*

What did you say?

I'm sorry. What?

What?

What was that?

Come again. (*folksy*)

Huh? (*informal or rude*)

Could you please repeat yourself?

Could you please repeat that?

122   When you do not understand what a foreign visitor has said

I don't understand you.

I can't understand you.

I can't hear you.

Please speak more slowly.

Could you please speak slower?

Could you please speak louder?

Could you write it down, please?

Please write it out.

Could you spell that?

TELLING TIME

123   Asking the time of day

What time is it?

Could you tell me what time it is?

Could you please tell me the time?

Could you give me the time?

Do you know what time it is?

Do you know the time?

Do you happen to have the time?

Do you have the correct time?

Do you have the time?

Could I bother you for the time?

124 The time is 12:00 o'clock
It's twelve noon.
It's noon.
It's twelve midnight.
It's midnight.

125 The time is on the hour
It's three.
It's three o'clock.
It's three o'clock sharp.
It's three o'clock on the dot.
It's three o'clock on the nose. (*informal*)
It's exactly three o'clock.

126 The time is approximate
It's almost three.
It's not quite three.
It's just after three.

127 The time is ten minutes past the hour
It's ten after three.
It's ten after.
It's ten minutes after three.
It's ten past three.
It's ten past.

128 The time is fifteen minutes past the hour
It's three fifteen.
It's a quarter past three.
It's three thirty.
It's half past three.
It's half past.

129 The time is forty minutes past the hour
It's three forty.

It's twenty of four.
It's twenty to four.
It's twenty till four.
It's twenty minutes till four.

130   The time is forty-five minutes past the hour
It's three forty-five.
It's quarter to four.
It's a quarter of four.
It's quarter to.
It's a quarter of.
It's a quarter till.
It's a quarter till four.

131   The time is fifty minutes past the hour
It's ten minutes to four.
It's ten to four.
It's ten to.
It's ten of.
It's ten till.

132   When a timepiece is not accurate
Is this clock right?
I think my watch needs a new battery.
This clock is fast.
This clock is slow.
My watch is running fast.
My watch has been running slow.

GENERAL PLEASANTRIES

133   When your moving about may bother someone
Excuse me.
Pardon me.
Coming through.

I beg your pardon.

Could I get by, please?

Watch your feet!

134 Offering to let someone enter in front of you

After you.

Ladies first.

You first.

Age before beauty. (*jocular cliché*)

Be my guest.

135 Apologizing to someone you have bothered

I'm sorry.

Forgive me.

Sorry to be a bother.

Sorry to be a pest.

Sorry for the inconvenience.

Please forgive the inconvenience.

136 Returning someone's good wishes

Same to you.

Likewise.

Likewise, I'm sure. (*cliché*)

Thank you.

137 Agreeing to something — polite

Of course.

Be happy to.

Fine.

Great.

Super. (*slang*)

138 Explaining that you will attend to someone soon

I'll be there in just a moment.

Be there in a minute.

I'll be right with you.

I'll be with you in a moment.

139 Asking for permission to leave a place — polite

Could I be excused?

May I be excused?

Might I be excused? (*formal*)

140 Saying good-bye — polite

Good afternoon.

Good evening.

Good morning.

Good day.

Good night.

Have a nice day.

Good-bye.

Bye.

Bye-bye.

Farewell.

Good-bye until later.

Good-bye until next time.

Good-bye for now.

141 Saying good-bye — informal

So long.

Ta-ta.

Farewell.

Cheerio.

See you later.

See you later, alligator. (*slang*)

Later, gator. (*slang*)

Later.

I'll try to catch you later.

I'll catch you later.

Catch you later.

See you.

See ya.

See you around.

Take care.

BUSINESS PLEASANTRIES

142   Announcing your arrival for an appointment

Mr. Smith to see Dr. Jones.

I'm here to see Mrs. Hodges.

Could you please tell Mr. Smith I'm here?

I have an appointment with Mrs. Jones.

143   Expressions used in business letters

We trust you will find the above to be of assistance.

We trust you will find everything in order.

Thank you for your attention to the above.

If there's anything you need, please don't hesitate to ask.

If we may be of further assistance, please don't hesitate to call.

Should you have any questions, please don't hesitate to call.

144   Being assertive — polite

I'd like my check now, please.

I'd like my payment now, please.

No, I don't think so.

> = *I totally reject your assertion.*

Excuse me?

> = *Did you really say what I think you said?*

May I have your name, please?

I'd like to speak to the manager.

I'd like to speak to your supervisor.

I intend to stand my ground.

I'm not leaving until I'm satisfied.

APOLOGIZING AND TAKING RESPONSIBILITY

145 Sincere apologies

Sorry.

So sorry.

I'm (so) very sorry.

I'm (so) sorry.

I'm really sorry.

I'm terribly sorry.

I'm sincerely sorry.

I apologize.

My apologies. (*formal*)

My sincere apologies. (*formal*)

You have my sincere apology. (*formal*)

Please accept my apology.

Please accept my apologies.

Please accept my heartfelt apology.

I offer my most sincere apology. (*formal*)

146 Offering a very polite apology

You cannot believe how sorry I am.

Words cannot describe how sorry I am.

I am just mortified.

Please send me the bill, and I'll take care of it.

147 Accepting the blame for something

It's my fault.

It's all my fault.

I'm fully responsible.

I take full responsibility.

I take the blame.

I blame no one but myself.

Mea culpa. (*Latin*)

> = *I am guilty.*

Mea maxima culpa. (*Latin*)

> = *I am completely guilty.*

148 Admitting your errors

My mistake.

I shouldn't have said that.

I shouldn't have done that.

I should have asked you first.

I didn't mean it.

I honestly didn't mean it.

I didn't mean it, honest.

I didn't mean to do it.

I didn't mean to do that.

I didn't mean to say that.

I didn't mean it that way.

I didn't intend it that way.

I don't know how that could have happened.

149 Promising never to repeat a particular mistake

It won't happen again.

It will never happen again.

I'll see (to it) that it never happens again.

I won't do it again.

150 Offering to make amends

How can I make it up to you?

How can I ever make it up to you?

Is there anything I can do (to make it up to you)?

I promise I'll make it up to you.

151 Asking for forgiveness

Please forgive me.

Can you forgive me?

Can you ever forgive me?

Can you find it in your heart to forgive me?

How can you ever forgive me?

I ask your forgiveness.

I beg your forgiveness. (*formal*)

I throw myself upon your mercy. (*formal*)

I ask for your mercy. (*formal*)

FORGIVING

152 Simple forgiveness

I forgive you.

You're forgiven.

All is forgiven.

That's all right.

It's okay. (*informal*)

That's okay. (*informal*)

Don't worry about it.

Think on it no more. (*formal*)

Think of it no more. (*formal*)

Think no more of it. (*formal*)

Don't give it another thought.

To err is human, to forgive divine. (*cliché*)

153 Forgiveness — informal

Forget it.

Forget about it.

Forgive and forget.

Don't worry about it.

Write it off.

I'll let you off this time.

I'll let it slide this time.

I'll give you another chance.

I'll turn the other cheek.

I won't hold it against you.

154 **Encouraging someone to end a dispute**
Let's drop the subject.

Let's bury the hatchet. (*idiomatic*)

Let's bring this matter to a close.

It's time to kiss and make up. (*cliché*)

SHOWING GRATITUDE

155 **Saying "thank you" — formal**
Thank you.

Thank you very much.

Thank you so much.

Thank you for your help.

Thank you for all you've done.

Thank you for everything.

You have my thanks.

You have my gratitude.

I'm deeply grateful.

I'm in your debt.

I'm indebted to you.

Thanks ever so much.

Thanks very much.

156 **Saying "thank you" — informal**
Thanks.

Thanks much.

Thanks for everything.

Thanks so much.

Thanks a lot.

Thanks a million.

Thanks a bunch.

Thanks a bundle.

Thanks heaps.

I owe you one.

I owe you big.

I owe you big-time.

RETURNING THANKS

157   **Acknowledging someone's thanks — formal**

You're welcome.

You're most welcome.

You're entirely welcome.

My pleasure.

It was my pleasure.

The pleasure was mine.

The pleasure was all mine.

The pleasure was entirely mine.

158   **Acknowledging someone's thanks — informal**

It was nothing.

Don't mention it.

No problem.

No sweat. (*slang*)

Any time.

No trouble.

No skin off my nose.

No skin off my teeth.

No skin off my back.

SPECIAL OCCASIONS

159   Seeing a new baby

Oh, isn't he cute!

Isn't he the sweetest thing!

Oh, isn't she darling!

She's beautiful.

She's so big!

What an adorable baby!

His eyes are just like his father's.

Her nose looks just like her mother's.

She has her father's eyes.

He's got his mother's nose.

160   Asking about a new baby

How much does he weigh?

Was he early?

Was she late?

What's his name?

Who is she named after?

Has he been sleeping well?

Is she sleeping through the night?

Does he sleep through the night yet?

Can I hold her?

May I hold him?

161   Congratulating someone for doing a good job

Congratulations!

Good going!

Good job!

Good work!

Bravo!

162 Wishing someone well

Happy Birthday!

. . . and many (many) more!

Many happy returns!

Happy Anniversary!

Congratulations!

Good luck!

Best wishes!

All our best!

Bon voyage! (*French*)

    (said when someone is leaving on a sea voyage)

Have a good time!

Have a good trip!

163 Expressing sympathy at a funeral or wake

I'm sorry.

I'm so sorry.

I'm very sorry.

You have my sympathy.

You have my deepest sympathy. (*formal*)

Please accept my sympathy. (*formal*)

My heart goes out to you.

I share your sorrow.

I share your pain.

How are you doing?

If you need anything, please let us know.

If there's anything we can do for you, please let us know.

You're in our prayers.

We'll keep you in our prayers.

IMPOLITE ENCOUNTERS

DEALING WITH UNPLEASANTNESS

164   When someone is conceited or vain

You're so vain.

You're too big for your britches. (*informal*)

    britches = trousers

You're getting a little big for your britches. (*informal*)

Aren't you getting a little big for your britches? (*informal*)

You're so full of yourself. (*idiomatic*)

You think you're pretty smart, don't you? (*informal*)

You think you're so smart. (*informal*)

You think you're so big. (*informal*)

You think you're such a big shot. (*informal*)

    a big shot = an important person

You love the sound of your own voice. (*informal*)

You just like to hear yourself talk. (*informal*)

You talk just to hear yourself speak. (*informal*)

You think the world revolves around you.

The world doesn't revolve around you.

You think you're the center of the universe.

You're all wrapped up in yourself.

All you think about is yourself.

Did you ever stop to think about anyone else?

165   When someone is overbearing

Who died and made you king? (*informal*)

Who died and made you Pope? (*informal*)

Who died and made you God? (*informal*)

Smarty. (*informal*)

Smart-ass. (*mildly vulgar*)

Smarty pants. (*slang*)

Know-it-all. (*informal*)

Get off your high horse. (*informal*)

    = *Be less arrogant.*

Who do you think you are?

You think you're so smart? (*informal*)

You and who else? (*informal*)

You and what army? (*slang*)

What makes you so special? (*informal*)

Don't break your arm patting yourself on the back.
   (*idiomatic*)

You think you're so hot. (*informal*)

   hot = important

You think you're such hot stuff. (*informal*)

   hot stuff = someone or something important

166   When someone has been insolent or rude — shocked response

The nerve of you!

   nerve = impudence; brashness

What nerve you have!

You have a lot of nerve!

You've got a lot of nerve!

The nerve!

You have a lot of gall!

   gall = nerve

The gall!

The very idea!

How dare you!

Why, I never!

How could you say such a thing?

How could you do such a thing?

I beg your pardon!

167 When someone has been insolent or rude — firm response

Don't get smart with me!

Don't get sassy with me. (*folksy*)

    sassy = insolent

Don't sass me. (*folksy*)

Don't talk back to me.

Don't give me any of your lip. (*informal*)

    lip = insolent talk

Don't get uppity on me. (*folksy*)

    uppity = arrogant

Don't get uppity with me. (*folksy*)

Don't get cocky. (*informal*)

    cocky = insolent

Don't get fresh. (*informal*)

    fresh = insolent; impudent

Don't get your nose out of joint. (*informal*)

Don't overstep your bounds.

Watch yourself.

Watch it. (*informal*)

Watch out. (*informal*)

168 When someone has been insolent or rude — rude response

Oh, a smart aleck? (*informal*)

    a smart aleck = an insolent person

Oh, a wiseguy? (*slang*)

    a wiseguy = a smart aleck

Oh, a wiseacre? (*slang*)

    a wiseacre = a smart aleck

Oh, a smart-ass? (*mildly vulgar*)

    a smart-ass = a smart aleck

Oh, a smart mouth? (*slang*)

    a smart mouth = an impudent-talking smart aleck

Wiseguy. (*slang*)

Wiseacre. (*slang*)

Smart aleck. (*informal*)

Smart-ass. (*mildly vulgar*)

Wipe that grin off your face. (*informal*)

Wipe that smirk off your face. (*informal*)

169 Encouraging a timid person

Show a little resolve.

Show some courage.

Show some spine.

Don't be so spineless.

Don't be such a chicken-shit. (*taboo*)
> *a chicken-shit = a coward*

Don't be such a lily-liver. (*informal*)
> *a lily-liver = a coward*

170 Insulting a coward

Chicken! (*slang*)
> *= Coward!*

Wimp! (*slang*)
> *= Coward!*

Wuss! (*slang*)
> *= Coward!*

Fraidy-cat! (*juvenile*)
> *a fraidy-cat = a coward*

Scaredy-cat! (*juvenile*)
> *a scaredy-cat = a coward*

You're yellow. (*informal*)
> *yellow = cowardly*

You yellow-bellied sapsucker. (*informal*)
> *= You coward.*

You are a gutless wonder. (*slang*)
> *gutless = cowardly*

You're afraid of your own shadow. (*informal*)

Are you a man or a mouse? (*cliché*)

Cat got your tongue? (*cliché*)

> = *Are you afraid or unable to speak?*

Got cold feet?

> = *Are you too frightened to act?*

You really wimped out. (*slang*)

> *wimped out* = *withdrew in a cowardly fashion*

You really chickened out. (*slang*)

> *chickened out* = *withdrew in a cowardly fashion*

Lose your nerve?

> = *Did you lose your resolve?*

171   When someone argues too much

Don't contradict me.

You see everything in black and white.

> *in black and white* = *in simple yes-no terms*

If I said it was black, you'd say it was white.

That's as different as day and night.

It's (the difference between) apples and oranges.

You're just being contrary.

You're just disagreeing to disagree.

You're just disagreeing for the sake of disagreeing.

You're just playing the devil's advocate.

You're just arguing for the sake of arguing.

You just like to hear yourself talk.

172   When someone is being annoying

Would you stop that?

Could you please stop doing that?

You are really trying my patience.

That's really annoying.

That's really irritating.

That's driving me nuts! (*slang*)

That's making me crazy! (*informal*)

That's really bothersome.

That's really bothering me.

That's really bugging me. (*slang*)

> *bugging = bothering*

That's getting on my nerves. (*idiomatic*)

> *getting on my nerves = annoying me*

That's grating on my nerves.

> *grating on my nerves = irritating me*

173 Inviting an annoying person to leave

Scram! (*slang*)

> = *Get out!; Go away!*

Get lost. (*slang*)

Go blow. (*slang*)

Go fry an egg. (*slang*)

Go suck a lemon. (*slang*)

Go take a long walk off a short pier. (*informal*)

Go take a long walk on a short pier. (*informal*)

Make yourself scarce. (*slang*)

Go away!

Go climb a tree! (*slang*)

Go fly a kite! (*slang*)

Go jump in the lake! (*informal*)

(Go) jump off a cliff. (*informal*)

Go play in traffic! (*informal*)

Buzz off! (*slang*)

Bug off! (*slang*)

Scat! (*slang*)

Scram! (*slang*)

Shoo! (*informal*)

Take a hike! (*slang*)

Make like a tree and leave. (*informal*)

Make like the wind and blow. (*informal*)

Get lost! (*slang*)

Get out of here! (*informal*)

Get out of my face! (*slang*)

Go blow. (*slang*)

Go play in traffic. (*informal*)

174 **When someone is very annoying or hurtful**

Why don't you rub a little salt in the wound?

Why don't you twist the knife in my back?

You're going to be the death of me yet.

You'd try the patience of a saint.

You really get my goat.

> *to get my goat = to annoy me*

You're driving me up a wall.

You're driving me up the wall.

You really know what buttons to push.

> *what buttons to push = how to make me angry*

You're pushing my buttons.

175 **Getting someone to stop doing something**

Must you (do that)?

Must you continue to do that?

Stop bothering me.

Stop pestering me.

Quit pestering me.

Give it a rest. (*slang*)

> *it = your mouth*

Knock it off! (*slang*)

Cut it out! (*slang*)

Enough, already! (*informal*)

176 **When someone is making you angry — rude**

I'm really upset with you right now.

Get a life! (*slang*)

Get a clue! (*slang*)

You're pissing me off. (*mildly vulgar*)

I'm really getting P.O.'d. (*mildly vulgar*)

    P.O.'d = pissed off = angry

177   Asking to be left alone

Let me be.

Let me alone.

Leave me be.

Please go away.

Please leave me alone.

I'm asking you to leave me alone.

I just want to be left alone.

178   Describing a bothersome person

You're a pain in the neck. (*slang*)

You're a pain in the ass. (*mildly vulgar*)

You're a pain in the butt. (*mildly vulgar*)

You're a royal pain. (*slang*)

You're a pain. (*slang*)

He grates on me.

He grates on my nerves.

    grates on my nerves = annoys me

He gets on my nerves.

He pushes my buttons.

He rubs me the wrong way.

He gets my dander up. (*informal*)

    dander = temper

He raises my hackles.

    hackles = long hairs at the back of the neck = temper

179   When someone has done something wrong — polite

How could you do such a silly thing?

How could you do such a thing?

What could you have been thinking?

What on earth were you thinking?

What possessed you to do that?

What got into you?

I hope you're sorry.

When will you ever learn?

Now what did you go and do that for? (*folksy*)

**180 When someone has done something wrong —
amazed**

Are you out of your mind?

Are you crazy?

Have you taken leave of your senses?

If I've told you once, I've told you a hundred times.
(*informal*)

If I've told you once, I've told you a thousand times.
(*informal*)

I can't believe you embarrassed me like that!

If that's what you think, you've got another think coming.
(*informal*)

You've got another thing coming. (*informal*)

**181 When someone has done something wrong —
sarcastic**

Are you happy (now)?

Are you satisfied?

I hope you're happy.

I hope you're satisfied.

Aren't you proud of yourself?

I hope you're proud of yourself.

182 When someone makes an unwelcome intervention

Who asked you? (*informal*)

Who asked your opinion?

When I want your opinion, I'll ask for it.

Who invited you?

You're not invited.

You're not welcome here.

We don't want your kind around here.

183 Telling someone to stay away or keep out

Keep out.

No trespassing.

Members only.

Employees only.

No admittance.

No admittance without proper identification. (*formal*)

These premises are for the use of members and guests
   only. (*formal*)

184 Asking someone's intentions

You got a problem? (*informal*)

What do you mean by that?

Were you talking to me?

Are you trying to start something?

(Just exactly) what are you getting at?

(Just exactly) what are you trying to say?

185 Starting a fight

Do you want to step outside (and settle this)?

Would you like to step outside?

Want to make something of it?

   something = an issue to fight about

Care to make something of it?

186 Asking someone to leave your property alone

Hands off!

Excuse me, that's mine.

Did I say you could touch that?

Look with your eyes not your hands.

If you break it, you pay for it.

If you break it, you've bought it.

187   Asking someone to stay out of your affairs

Mind your own business. (*informal*)

Mind your own beeswax. (*slang*)

> *beeswax* = *business*

M.Y.O.B. (*slang*)

> = *Mind your own business.*

Butt out! (*slang*)

> = *Mind your own business!*

That's none of your affair.

Get your nose out of my business. (*informal*)

Keep your nose out of my business. (*informal*)

188   When someone is harassing you — angry and direct

Get off my back! (*slang*)

Lay off, will you! (*slang*)

Get off my tail! (*slang*)

Get off my ass! (*mildly vulgar*)

Get off it! (*slang*)

Come off it! (*slang*)

189   When someone is harassing you — rude

Nuts to you. (*mildly vulgar*)

Screw you. (*mildly vulgar*)

Up yours. (*vulgar*)

190   When someone is presumptuous

Why would you ask such a thing?

How could you say such a thing?

What right do you have to say that?

Who gave you the right?

Where do you come off saying that?

Well, I never!

191   When someone has underestimated your intelligence

How dumb do you think I am? (*informal*)

Do you think I was born yesterday? (*informal*)

Who do you think you're kidding? (*informal*)

Who do you think you're talking to? (*informal*)

192   When someone interrupts with an opinion

Was I talking to you?

Who asked you?

I wasn't speaking to you.

When I want your opinion, I'll ask it.

When I want your opinion, I'll beat it out of you. (*jocular*)

Thank you for sharing. (*sarcastic*)

I'll thank you to keep your opinions to yourself.

I'll thank you to mind your own business!

Keep your nose out of my business. (*informal*)

Keep your opinions to yourself.

Mind your own business.

Mind your own beeswax. (*slang*)

    beeswax = business

M.Y.O.B. (*slang*)

    = *Mind your own business.*

193   Apologizing — sarcastic

Well, excuse me. (*informal*)

Excuse me for breathing. (*informal*)

Excuse me for living. (*informal*)

Pardon me for living. (*informal*)

194 When someone overreacts

Relax.

Don't get bent out of shape. (*slang*)

Don't make a federal case out of it. (*informal*)

Like it's such a big deal. (*informal*)

It's no big deal. (*informal*)

You're making a mountain out of a molehill.

Don't bite my head off. (*informal*)

Don't jump down my throat. (*informal*)

Same to you. (*informal*)

So's your uncle. (*informal*)

Sue me. (*informal*)

So, sue me. (*informal*)

195 When punishment is in store for someone

You'll get yours.

You'll get your due.

You'll get what's coming to you.

What goes around comes around. (*cliché*)

You'll get your just deserts.

196 Explaining harsh justice

What goes around comes around. (*cliché*)

It cuts both ways. (*cliché*)

Quid pro quo. (*Latin*)

   = *This for that.*

An eye for an eye; a tooth for a tooth.

The chickens have come home to roost.

Two can play (at) that game. (*informal*)

Serves you right.

197 Threatening retaliation

I'll give you a dose of your own medicine. (*cliché*)

I'll fix your wagon. (*cliché*)

I dare you.

Go ahead, make my day. (*cliché*)

198   Requesting silence

Quiet!

Be quiet!

Keep quiet!

Keep still!

Be still!

Hush!

Silence! (*formal*)

Shut up! (*informal*)

Shut your mouth! (*informal*)

Shut your trap! (*informal*)

Hold your tongue!

Hush your mouth! (*informal*)

Shush! (*informal*)

Shh! (*informal*)

Not another word!

Button your lip! (*informal*)

Clam up! (*slang*)

Dry up! (*slang*)

199   Requesting someone to stop needless talk

Can it! (*slang*)

Stow it! (*slang*)

Put a cork in it! (*slang*)

   it = your mouth

Put a sock in it! (*slang*)

Cut the gab! (*slang*)

   gab = needless chatter

Cut the crap! (*mildly vulgar*)

   crap = dung = needless chatter

200   When someone is not doing enough

You're not doing your share.

You're not doing your fair share.

You're not carrying your weight.

You're not pulling your weight.

You're not pulling your own weight.

You're not living up to your end of the bargain.

You're not holding up your end of the bargain.

You're not reaching your potential.

You're slacking off.

Get on the stick. (*slang*)

201   When someone starts trouble

Stop stirring things up.

You like to make trouble, don't you?

Don't you have anything better to do?

You've got too much time on your hands.

Can't you leave well enough alone?

Get a job! (*slang*)

Get a hobby! (*informal*)

Get a life! (*slang*)

202   Expressing mock sympathy

Aw, poor baby.

You poor thing.

My heart bleeds for you.

I'm all choked up.

203   Expressing mock sympathy — sarcastic

Here's a quarter. Call someone who cares.

Obviously you've mistaken me for someone who cares.

What makes you think I care?

Do you think I care?

Like I care. (*informal*)
As if I care. (*informal*)
As if. (*informal*)
Frankly, my dear, I don't give a damn. (*mildly vulgar*)
Good for you.
I'm happy for you.
Thanks for sharing.
I'm so glad you told us that.
Thank you for sharing.
Isn't that special?

204   When you are helpless to help — rude
What do you want me to do about it?
What do you expect me to do about it?
What am I supposed to do about it?
Like I can do anything about it.

GUESTS AND HOSTS

205   Asking to visit someone

Are you free later today?

Could I come over later today?

Can I come over?

Do you mind if I stop by later today?

Would you mind if I stopped by later?

Would it be a problem if I dropped by for a few minutes?

Would it be all right if I dropped by for a few minutes?

Are you busy or can I come over?

When would be a good time for me to come over?

When's a good time for you?

I'll be there by seven.

I'll be there after dinner.

206   When you are invited to an informal meal in a home

Do I need to bring anything?

Would you like me to bring anything?

Can I bring something?

Can I bring anything?

Should I bring anything?

What should I bring?

Would you like me to bring wine?

Shall I bring wine?

I'll bring the wine.

Let me bring dessert.

207   Asking about an invitation you have received
What time should I be there?
What do you have planned?
How should I dress?
What should I wear?
Is it casual or formal?
I'm planning to drive. How's the parking?
Can I bring my kids?
May I bring a friend?
Can I bring something?
    something = food

208   Apologizing for being late
I'm sorry I'm late.
Sorry I'm late.
I'm sorry to have kept you waiting.
Sorry to have kept you waiting.

209   Explaining why one is late
I misjudged the time.
I didn't realize it was so late.
I lost track of time.
I overslept.
My alarm didn't go off.
I got a late start.
I got sidetracked.
    sidetracked = detoured; distracted
My last appointment ran over.
I had to run an errand.
I had to drop someone off.
I had to get money.
I couldn't get a taxi.
I couldn't get a cab.

The train was late.

The bus was late.

I missed the bus.

I missed my ride.

My ride didn't show (up).

I had to get gas.

I had to stop for gas.

I had to stop and get gas.

I ran out of gas.

Traffic was slow.

Traffic was hell. (*mildly vulgar*)

I was stuck in traffic.

I got lost.

I missed my exit.

There was construction.

There was an accident.

It took me longer to get here than I thought it would.

It took longer than I expected to get here.

I didn't realize this was so far away.

It was further than I thought.

I was looking for parking.

I couldn't find a parking spot.

I couldn't find a parking place.

I couldn't find a place to park.

210 When you finally arrive after being late

I hope you started without me.

I'm glad you started without me.

Were you waiting long?

You should have started without me.

Next time start without me.

211 Greetings for visitors

Look who's here!

Well, look who's here!

Am I surprised to see you!

Am I ever surprised to see you!

Look at what the cat dragged in! (*folksy*)

Fancy meeting you here.

212 Inviting a visitor to come in

Come on in.

Come right on in.

Come right in.

Do come in. (*formal*)

Please come in.

Come in and relax for a few minutes.

Come in and take a load off your feet. (*folksy*)

Come in and take a load off. (*folksy*)

Come in and sit down.

Come in and set a spell. (*folksy*)

Come in and stay a while.

Come in and make yourself at home.

213 After greeting a visitor

To what do I owe the pleasure of this unexpected visit?
   (*formal*)

To what do I owe this visit?

What are you doing here?

What brings you here?

What brings you to this neck of the woods? (*folksy*)

   neck of the woods = location

Why this delightful surprise?

What a delightful surprise!

What a nice surprise!

It's nice to see you again.

It's a pleasure to see you again. (*formal*)

It's so good to see you again.

It's so good to see you after all this time.

Good seeing you again.

I'm delighted to have you visit.

I'm delighted to have you.

Delighted to have you here.

I'm so happy you looked me up.

I'm so glad you looked me up.

I'm so glad you took the trouble to look me up.

I'm so glad you could come.

I'm so glad you could come by.

I'm so glad you could make it.

I'm so glad you could drop by.

I'm so glad you could stop by.

I'm so glad you could visit.

Glad you could come.

Glad you could drop by.

Glad you could stop by.

We've wanted to have you over before this.

We've wanted to invite you over before this.

We've been meaning to have you over.

We've been meaning to invite you over.

We've been looking forward to seeing you for a long time.

We've been wanting to see you for a long time.

214 Making a visitor feel welcome and comfortable

Make yourself comfortable.

Make yourself comfy.

Make yourself right at home.

Make yourself at home.

Would you like to take off your coat?

Here, let me take your coat.

Can I take your coat and hat?

Can I help you off with your things?

Let me help you off with your things.

Take your coat off and stay awhile.

Why don't you take off your coat and make yourself comfortable?

Put your things anywhere and sit down for a minute.

Just drop your coat here. (*informal*)

215 Inviting a visitor to stay for dinner

Can you stay for dinner?

> *Can you* ≈ *Would you, Are you able to, Will you*

Can you have dinner with us?

Can you stay and have dinner with us?

Would you care to stay for dinner?

216 Encouraging a guest to feel at home

Please make yourself at home.

Our house is your house.

My house is your house.

If there's anything you need, don't hesitate to ask.

If there's anything you want, don't hesitate to ask.

If there's anything I can do for you, just ask.

You're to do exactly as you please.

Please do exactly as you please.

Would you like to freshen up a bit?

Would you like something to drink?

Can I get you something to drink?

217 Offering a guest a seat

Please sit down.

Have a seat.

Try this chair. It's more comfortable.

Would you like to sit over here?

Would you prefer a more comfortable chair?

218 Steering a guest to a particular room

Please come into the living room.

Come on in the living room.

Right this way. Everyone seems to be in the kitchen.

The other guests are in the library.

Would you like to join us in the living room?

Everyone is in the living room. Would you care to join us?

219 Encouraging a guest to be independent

Please go around and introduce yourself to everyone.

Can you just introduce yourself to the other guests?

Just go in and meet everyone.

I hope you don't mind introducing yourself around.

Don't stand on ceremony. Make yourself known.

Get yourself a drink and something to eat.

Please feel free to mingle with the other guests.

I hope you don't mind getting yourself a drink.

The bar's over there. Please help yourself.

220 Mingling with other guests

Mind if I join you?

Care if I join you?

May I join you?

Hello, my name is Bill.

Hello, I'm Jane.

So how do you know John and Mary?

I work with John.

I'm friends with Mary.

I'm a friend of Mary's.

Have you tried the dip?

Great party, huh? (*informal*)

What a great spread!

> *spread = display of party food*

221   What a guest says to a host or hostess
Where can I put my coat?
Do you mind if I smoke?
Mind if I smoke?
Where is the bathroom(, please)?
You have a beautiful home.
The table looks beautiful.
I love what you have done with the living room.
You have a wonderful place.
You have wonderful taste.

222   Starting a conversation using the topic of weather
Nice weather we're having.
Lousy weather, isn't it?
Horrible weather we're having.
Lovely weather for ducks. (*sarcastic*)
It's raining again.
Hot enough for you? (*ironic*)
Cold enough for you? (*ironic*)
It's not the heat; it's the humidity. (*cliché*)

223   Asking a question to start a conversation
What's new?
What's up?
What time is it?
Do you have the time?
This food is good, isn't it?

224   Starting a conversation with someone you know well
How have you been?
How's work?
How's your family?
How's the family?

Looks like you just got a haircut.

I like your hair.

I like your outfit.

That dress is lovely.

That dress looks nice on you.

Where did you buy that sweater? I've been wanting to get one.

225   Starting a conversation in a waiting room

Can I take a look at your paper?

What are you listening to?

What book are you reading?

Read any good books lately?

Did you see that show last night?

Do you have a cigarette?

Do you have a breath mint?

I'm going to get a coffee. Would you like one?

226   Talking about the weather

Nice weather we're having.

The sun is shining.

It's bright and sunny.

It's eighty degrees.

Lousy weather, huh?

Horrible weather we're having.

Lovely weather for ducks. (*sarcastic*)

It's not the heat; it's the humidity. (*cliché*)

It's raining again.

It's raining cats and dogs. (*cliché*)

What a storm!

What a downpour!

What a snowstorm!

What a blizzard!

Hot enough for you? (*ironic*)

Cold enough for you? (*ironic*)

It's raining.

It's snowing.

It's cold.

It's hot.

It's humid.

It's foggy.

It's smoggy.

It's muggy.

It's windy.

227 What to say when in a crowded place

It's too crowded in here.

I feel like a sardine.

We're packed in like sardines.

We're crammed in like sardines.

We're crammed solid.

This party is wall-to-wall people.

It's absolutely jam-packed.

I'm getting claustrophobic.

I need some elbowroom.

There's no room to breathe.

There's not enough room to swing a cat. (*folksy*)

228 Preparing to leave home

Do we have everything?

Have we forgotten anything?

Did we forget anything?

Do you have your keys?

Did you leave a light on?

I can't find my keys.

Wait, I forgot my wallet.

Did you bring the map?

Do you have the directions?

Are the kids ready?
Is the answering machine on?
Did you go to the bathroom?
Did you unplug the iron?
Did you turn off the TV?
Did you turn off the stove?

229 Stating when you will return home
I'll be gone just a few minutes.
See you in an hour.
I won't be late.
I'll be back by ten.
I'll be home late.
Don't wait up for me.

230 Preparing to leave a host or hostess
Well, it's getting late.
Is it that late already?
Is it that time already?
Looks like it's that time.
The time has come.
I hate to eat and run.
I don't want to wear out my welcome.
I need my beauty sleep. (*jocular*)
We have to get up early tomorrow.
We have a big day tomorrow.
   big = busy
I need to run.
I'm afraid I must run.
I'm afraid I must be going.
I've got to be running.
I'm afraid I have to be going.
I've got to be going.

I'd better be off.

I'd best be off.

I'd best leave now.

I better get moving.

I better hit the road.

I must be off.

I must say good night.

I've got to hit the road. (*idiomatic*)

I better get on my horse. (*idiomatic*)

I'm off. (*informal*)

I'm out of here. (*slang*)

I'm history. (*slang*)

Better be going.

Better be off.

Better get moving.

Better hit the road. (*idiomatic*)

Time to call it a day.

Time to call it a night.

Time to go.

Time to run.

Time to hit the road.

Time to move along.

Time to push along.

Time to push off.

Time to shove off.

Time to split. (*slang*)

Time flies when you're having fun. (*cliché*)

Gotta go.

Got to hit the road.

Got to run.

Got to shove off.

Got to split. (*slang*)

Got to take off.

Got to be shoving off.
Got to fly.
Got to get moving.
Got to go home and get my beauty sleep. (*jocular*)
Have to be moving along.
Have to go now.
Have to move along.
Have to run along.
Have to shove off.

231   When departing

Thanks for having me over.
Thank you for a lovely evening. (*formal*)
Thank you for a lovely time. (*formal*)
Thank you for having us.
Thank you for inviting us.

232   Questions asked of departing guests

Do you want a cup of coffee before you go?
Are you sober enough to drive?
Can I call you a taxi?
Can you find your way home?
Will you get home all right?
Will you get home okay? (*informal*)
Do you have everything?
>   *everything = everything that you arrived with*

233   Saying good-bye to departing guests

It's been a delightful visit. (*formal*)
It's been delightful.
It's been our pleasure.
So good to see you.
Do you have everything?
Thank you for coming.

Thanks for coming.

Thanks for dropping in.

Thanks for dropping by.

Thanks for stopping over.

I'm so glad you stopped by.

Glad you could come.

Glad you could drop by.

Glad you could stop by.

Come back soon.

Come back anytime.

Come back when you can stay longer.

Do come back soon.

Let's do this again soon.

We have to do this again sometime.

See you soon.

MISCELLANEOUS EXPRESSIONS

COMMENTS AND PHRASES

234   **General exclamations**

Wow!

Gosh!

Golly!

Gee!

Gee whiz!

Gee willikers!

Holy cow!

Holy smoke!

Holy Toledo!

Son of a gun!

Son of a bitch! (*mildly vulgar*)

Son of a bucket!

Son of a sea biscuit!

Well, I'll be!

I'll be darned!

I'll be damned! (*mildly vulgar*)

Well, I'll be a monkey's uncle!

What do you know?

Imagine that!

Can you beat that!

Fancy that!

Isn't that something!

Well if that ain't the cats' meow.

By gum! (*folksy*)

By golly! (*folksy*)

By Jove!

By George!

Great Scott!

Oh, my!

My word!

Oh, my goodness!

My goodness!

Goodness!

Heavens!

Good heavens!

For heaven's sake!

For Pete's sake!

For pity's sake!

Good gracious!

Good grief!

Goodness gracious!

My God! (*oath*)

Oh my God! (*oath*)

God forbid! (*mild oath*)

Great!

Excellent!

Hot dog!

Hot diggety! (*folksy*)

Good Lord!

Hot damn! (*mildly vulgar*)

Lordy! (*mild oath*)

Lordy be! (*mild oath*)

Lord have mercy! (*mild oath*)

Saints preserve us! (*mild oath*)

Glory be!

Hush my mouth! (*folksy*)

Shut my mouth! (*folksy*)

As I live and breathe!

My stars!

Zounds!

Gadzooks!

You don't say!

Will wonders never cease!

235 Religious expressions

Amen!

> = *I agree!*

Hallelujah!

> = *Hooray!*

Alleluia!

> = *Hooray!*

Hosanna!

> = *Hooray!*

Glory (be) to God!

Praise be to God!

Thanks be to God.

236 Expressions meaning "almost"

Nice try. (*sarcastic*)

Not quite.

So near and yet so far.

So close and yet so far.

Close, but no cigar. (*cliché*)

You were within a hair's breadth.

Close enough for government work. (*informal*)

Almost only counts in horseshoes and hand grenades.
(*cliché*)

It's all or nothing.

A miss is as good as a mile. (*cliché*)

237 Expressing death

She died.

She's deceased.

She perished. (*formal*)

She expired. (*formal*)

She passed on. (*euphemistic*)

She passed away. (*euphemistic*)

He's no longer among us.

He's not among the living.

She's gone to a better land.

She's gone to heaven.

She's with the angels.

She's joined the angels in heaven. (*euphemistic*)

She's gone to meet her maker.

She met her maker.

She's with her maker.

The Lord took her home. (*euphemistic*)

He went west. (*euphemistic*)

He quit this world. (*euphemistic*)

She kicked the bucket. (*slang*)

He kicked off. (*slang*)

She kicked. (*slang*)

He bit the big one. (*slang*)

He bit the dust. (*slang*)

She dropped dead. (*informal*)

She bought the farm. (*slang*)

She bought the ranch. (*slang*)

She's six feet under. (*informal*)

He's pushing up daisies. (*informal*)

She croaked. (*slang*)

238   Leaving things as they are

Let it be.

Leave it be.

Let it go.

Let things be.

Live and let live.

239

If it ain't broke, don't fix it. (*cliché*)
Let sleeping dogs lie. (*cliché*)
Don't make waves. (*idiomatic*)
Don't rock the boat. (*idiomatic*)
Don't make trouble.
Don't go looking for trouble.

239   Expressing differences between people — clichés
Different strokes for different folks.
One man's meat is another man's poison.
One man's trash is another man's treasure.
Tastes differ.
There's no accounting for taste.
Variety is the spice of life.
It takes all kinds.
It takes all kinds to make a world.
Vive la difference! (*French*)
    = *Hooray for the difference!*

240   Warnings
Be prepared!
Be careful!
Watch out!
Watch it!
Look out!
Look sharp!
Watch your step!
Heads up!
Behind you!
To your right!
On your left!
Coming through!
Gangway!

Make way!

Fore!

> *(said in golfing when the ball is struck)*

Duck!

Hit the pavement!

Hit the deck!

Beware!

Caution!

Proceed with caution.

Man overboard!

> *(said when someone falls from a boat into the water)*

Fire!

Take care.

Safety first.

Look before you leap.

Let's take this one step at a time. (*cliché*)

Leave nothing to chance. (*cliché*)

Slow down.

Take your time.

Play it cool.

Play it safe.

Don't blow your cover.

Stop, look, and listen.

Look both ways before you cross the street.

Let the buyer beware.

Caveat emptor. (*Latin*)

> = *Let the buyer beware.*

We're not out of the woods yet. (*idiomatic*)

We're skating on thin ice.

241 On disappearance

He vanished.

He just disappeared.

It just disappeared.

He disappeared without a trace.

It was gone without a trace.

He was gone with the wind. (*cliché*)

Poof! He was gone. (*informal*)

One minute she was there and the next minute she wasn't.

Now, where did he disappear to?

Now, where's he gotten to? (*folksy*)

Now, where did he run off to? (*folksy*)

242   Giving and receiving — clichés

What goes around, comes around.

You scratch my back, I'll scratch yours.

One hand washes the other.

Do unto others as you would have them do unto you.

Do as you would be done by.

As a man sows, so shall he reap.

Tit for tat.

> = *This in return for that.*

Quid pro quo. (*Latin*)

> = *Tit for tat.*

243   Cause and effect — clichés

April showers bring May flowers.

You made your bed; now lie in it.

As the twig is bent, so is the tree inclined.

As the twig is bent, so grows the tree.

One good turn deserves another.

One thing leads to another.

244   Saying the obvious — clichés

It's not over 'til it's over.

Boys will be boys.

East is east, west is west.

That's that.

Life is life.

Enough is enough.

245 Expressions for a forgotten word or name

Whatsit.

Whaddya call it.

Whatchamacallit.

Whatchamajig.

Thingamajig.

Thingamajigger.

What's 'er name.

What's 'is name.

What's 'is face.

What's 'er face.

You know who.

You know what I mean.

That certain something.

Je ne sais quoi. (*French*)

   = *I don't know.*

246 Regarding order and procedure

There is a time and a place for everything. (*cliché*)

A place for everything and everything in its place. (*cliché*)

Everything has its season. (*cliché*)

All in due time. (*cliché*)

First things first. (*cliché*)

First come, first served. (*cliché*)

The first shall be last and the last shall be first. (*Biblical*)

Rules are made to be broken. (*cliché*)

Rules are meant to be followed, not broken.

When in Rome, do as the Romans do. (*cliché*)

Don't put the cart before the horse. (*cliché*)

Don't count your chickens before they are hatched. (*cliché*)

Let's cross that bridge when we come to it. (*cliché*)

Do what you are told.

Do as you are told.

I just do what I am told.

I just do as I am told.

I just work here.

Follow the rules.

That's how we do it here.

Go by the book.

You must go through proper channels.

247 Describing a messy place

This place is a mess.

This place is a pigsty.

This place is a disgrace.

What a mess.

What a pit. (*slang*)

What a dump. (*slang*)

What a junk heap. (*slang*)

This place looks like a tornado hit it.

This place looks like a national disaster (area).

This place looks like a disaster area.

This place looks like it went through the war.

This place looks like it's been through a war.

This place looks like it's been through World War III.

How can you find anything in here?

How do you expect to find anything in this mess?

Were you raised in a barn?

How about cleaning up a little around here?

If you would put things where they belong, they wouldn't get lost.

248   Concerning unity — clichés

United we stand; divided we fall.

A house divided against itself cannot stand.

All for one and one for all.

Birds of a feather flock together.

Many hands make light work.

249   Concerning nostalgia

When I was a kid . . .

When I was your age . . .

In my day . . .

In my time . . .

In that day and age . . .

Those were the days.

Those were the good old days.

They don't make them like they used to.

250   Concerning strength — clichés

You don't know your own strength.

You're as strong as an ox.

A chain is only as strong as its weakest link.

251   Concerning rigidity of character — idioms and clichés

He's set in his ways.

A leopard cannot change his spots.

You can't teach an old dog new tricks.

Old habits die hard.

You're as stubborn as a bull.

Why are you so bullheaded?

252   Feeling warm or hot

It's hot in here.

It's like an oven in here.

I'm sweltering.

I'm going to melt.

Open a window.

Turn on the air-conditioner.

Hot enough for you? (*ironic*)

Is it hot enough for you? (*ironic*)

It's not the heat, it's the humidity. (*cliché*)

It's as hot as hell. (*mildly vulgar*)

253   Feeling cool or cold

It's cold in here.

I'm freezing.

I'm shivering.

My teeth are chattering.

My lips are blue.

I'm going numb.

I'm chilled to the bone.

Shut the window.

Turn on the heat.

Turn up the heat.

Turn the heat up.

Cold enough for you? (*ironic*)

Is it cold enough for you? (*ironic*)

254   Describing additional unspecified people or things

Et cetera. (*Latin*)

= *And so forth.*

And so on.

And so forth.

And everything.

And everything else.

And everything like that.

And all like that.

And stuff. (*slang*)
And stuff like that (there). (*slang*)
And what have you.
And like that.
And then some.

255 Concerning whiteness

It was white as snow.
Her skin was white as alabaster.
Her skin was like alabaster.
You're as pale as a ghost.
You're white as a ghost.

256 Concerning blackness

It's pitch black.
It's black as night.
It's black as coal.
I can't see my hand in front of my face.

257 Concerning cleanliness

It's as clean as a whistle.
It's so clean you could eat off the floor.
It's spic and span.
Clean your room.
Pick up your clothes.
I want you to pick up your room.
I want this place spotless.
Pick up after yourself.
Were you raised in a barn?
You live like a pig!
A place for everything, and everything in its place.
    (*cliché*)
Cleanliness is next to godliness. (*cliché*)

258 Concerning surprise

Unbelievable!

I had no idea!

Who would have thought?

It was the last thing I expected.

I never would have guessed.

I was caught unaware.

I was caught unawares. (*informal*)

It was the shock of my life.

It dropped like a bomb.

It dropped from the clouds.

It appeared from the clouds.

It burst onto the scene.

It came out of left field.

It came from nowhere.

It appeared out of nowhere.

It came from out of the blue.

It was a bolt from the blue.

It threw me for a loop.

That knocked me for a loop.

You could have knocked me over with a feather. (*cliché*)

259 Concerning expectation

It came as no surprise.

I knew it was coming.

It's just as I expected.

My fingers are crossed.

I'm crossing my fingers.

I'm waiting with bated breath. (*cliché*)

I'll wait for you.

I'll stay up for you.

I'll wait up.

I'll sit up and wait.

260 **Concerning a premonition**

I have a hunch.

I have a feeling.

I just have this feeling.

I get the feeling something's going to happen.

I feel it in my bones.

I can feel it.

I can sense it.

My sixth sense tells me that . . .

My gut tells me that . . .

It's women's intuition.

A storm is brewing.

The handwriting's on the wall. (*cliché*)

It's an omen.

It's a harbinger of things to come.

It's a sign of things to come.

It's a portent of things to come.

It's a good sign.

It's a bad sign.

It's a good omen.

It's a bad omen.

261 **Concerning being busy — clichés**

You're as busy as a beaver.

You're as busy as a bee.

Many hands make light work.

A little work never hurt anyone.

It's all in a day's work.

A woman's work is never done.

All work and no play makes Jack a dull boy.

God helps those who help themselves.

262   Making an extra effort

I've gone out of my way to please you.

I've bent over backwards for you.

I've gone the extra mile.

I've gone beyond the call of duty.

I've gone above and beyond the call of duty.

You've gotten the royal treatment.

I've treated you like a king.

I've treated you like a queen.

We've rolled out the red carpet. (*idiomatic*)

> = *We've prepared for the event as if we were preparing for royalty.*

You're getting the red-carpet treatment. (*idiomatic*)

> *red-carpet = royal*

We aim to please.

We aim to treat you right. (*folksy*)

263   Demanding to be given an object

Give it to me.

Give it here. (*informal*)

Give it up. (*informal*)

Gimme it. (*informal*)

Gimme. (*informal*)

Give. (*informal*)

Cough it up. (*informal*)

> *it = money*

Hand it over. (*informal*)

Fork it over. (*slang*)

Let me have it.

Where is it?

Leave it go. (*informal*)

Let it go.

Let go of that.

264 When someone is preparing for an important event — clichés

This is your big night.

This could be your lucky day.

This is it.

This is the moment you've been waiting for.

This is the big moment.

Knock 'em dead. (*informal*)

Break a leg. (*informal*)

> (*a way of wishing good luck to an actor before a performance*)

Make us proud of you.

Make us proud.

I'm sure you will make us proud of you.

265 When someone is dressed up

You're dressed to the nines. (*slang*)

You're dressed to kill. (*slang*)

You're all dressed up.

You're all gussied up. (*informal*)

> *gussied up = dressed up (male or female)*

You're all dolled up. (*informal*)

> *dolled up = dressed up like a doll (male or female)*

You look great in a monkey suit. (*informal*)

> *monkey suit = tuxedo; evening jacket (usually male)*

You look like a million bucks.

You look like a million dollars.

You look like a million.

You look a million.

266 When you feel you are not wanted

Do you want me to go (away)?

Do you want me to leave?

Would you like me to leave?

If you want me to leave, just ask.

If you want me to leave, why don't you just say so?

I know when I'm not wanted.

I don't like being here any better than you do.

Am I cramping your style? (*informal*)

267 Regarding something less than what was desired

I was hoping for more.

I was counting on more.

I was gunning for more.

It's not what I had in mind.

It's not what I pictured.

It's not what I hoped for.

It's not what I had hoped for.

It's not what I expected.

It's not what I anticipated.

I expected something more.

It's a far cry from what I expected.

It leaves a lot to be desired.

They got the best of me.

I've been cheated.

I didn't get what I bargained for.

I was taken advantage of.

I got left holding the bag.

> *I got ≈ I've been, I was*

I got gypped. (*informal*)

> *gypped = cheated*

I got rooked. (*informal*)

> *rooked = cheated*

I got the short end of the stick.

> *the short end of the stick = the losing part of a bargain*

I got robbed. (*informal*)

I got taken. (*informal*)

I got taken to the cleaners. (*informal*)

I got a bum deal. (*informal*)

    a bum deal = a bad deal; an unfair deal

I got a raw deal. (*informal*)

    a raw deal = a bad deal; an unfair deal

I got screwed. (*mildly vulgar*)

268   Describing a reprimand

I got chewed out. (*informal*)

    I got ≈ I've been, I was

I got my ass chewed out. (*mildly vulgar*)

I got raked over the coals. (*idiomatic*)

I got hauled over the coals. (*idiomatic*)

I got an earful.

I was put through the wringer.

I was taken to task.

They let me off the hook this time. (*idiomatic*)

    off the hook = free from an obligation or guilt

They let me off easy.

They let me off with just a warning.

They let it slide.

They let it go.

I just got a slap on the wrist.

    a slap on the wrist = a mild punishment

269   When something is broken

It broke.

It's broken.

It doesn't work.

It's on the fritz. (*idiomatic*)

    on the fritz = out of order

It's on the blink. (*informal*)

    on the blink = out of order

This thing is really screwed up! (*informal*)

    screwed up = messed up; made to be out of order

270   **When something is out of order**

It's out of order.

It's out of service.

It's out of kilter. (*informal*)

It's out of whack. (*informal*)

It's dead. (*informal*)

It's kaput. (*slang*)

    kaput (German) = dead

It up and died (on me). (*folksy*)

It died on me.

It's in the shop.

    in the shop = in the repair shop

It's out of commission.

271   **On being pushed to the limit of your patience**

That's the straw that broke the camel's back. (*cliché*)

    = That's the minor thing that will finally trigger some activity.

That's the last straw! (*cliché*)

    the last straw = the straw that broke the camel's back

That does it!

That's it.

I've had it.

That tears it. (*idiomatic*)

This is too much.

This is more than I can bear.

This is more than I can take.

This is more than I can stand.

That's just what I needed.

I needed that like a hole in the head. (*sarcastic*)

That's a fine how-do-you-do.

Here's a fine how-do-you-do.

Well, that takes the cake! (*idiomatic*)

That's just swell! (*sarcastic*)

That's just great! (*sarcastic*)

Now what?

 = *What else could possibly happen at this point?*

PERSONAL MATTERS

FEELINGS

272 **Asking if someone is all right**

Are you OK?

Are you all right?

Are you feeling OK?

Life got you down? (*informal*)

Are things getting you down?

You look like you lost your best friend. (*cliché*)

You look like the wind has been taken out of your sails.
(*idiomatic*)

273 **Asking why someone looks so unhappy**

What's the matter?

Something got you down?

What's got you down?

Why are you so blue?

> *blue = sad*

Why is your face so long?

> *face so long = face so sad*

Who rained on your parade? (*idiomatic*)

> *rained on your parade = ruined your plans*

What rained on your parade? (*idiomatic*)

Did someone rain on your parade? (*idiomatic*)

Who burst your bubble? (*idiomatic*)

> *= Who ruined your good outlook on life?*

274 **Offering someone help and advice**

Would you like to talk about it?

Need someone to talk to?

If you need someone to talk to, I'm always available.

I'm here if you want to talk about it.

275 Encouraging someone who is unhappy

Cheer up!

Things are never as bad as they seem.

It will (all) work out.

Don't let it get you down. (*idiomatic*)

Chin up. (*cliché*)

Keep your chin up. (*cliché*)

Things will get better.

Tomorrow is another day. (*cliché*)

It's always darkest before dawn. (*cliché*)

Stop carrying the weight of the world on your shoulders.

There's no point in carrying the weight of the world on your shoulders.

276 When you are depressed

I'm depressed.

> *I'm ≈ He's, She's, They're, We're, Tom's, Jane's, etc.*

I'm feeling low.

I'm feeling down.

I'm feeling blue. (*idiomatic*)

> *blue = sad*

I'm out of sorts.

I'm in the doldrums.

I'm a little down in the mouth. (*idiomatic*)

I'm down in the dumps.

> *= I am depressed.*

I've been down in the dumps lately.

I can't put my finger on what's wrong.

277 Expressing despair and emptiness

My heart is heavy.

> *My ≈ Her, His, Our, Jane's, Tom's, etc.*

My heart is broken.

I'm downhearted.

> *I'm ≈ He's, She's, They're, We're, Tom's, Jane's, etc.*

I'm broken-hearted.

I'm heartbroken.

278 When someone looks very happy

You look like you just won the jackpot.

You look like you died and went to heaven.

You're looking on top of the world.

What're you smiling about?

279 When someone is very happy — idioms

I'm on Cloud Nine.

> *I'm ≈ He's, She's, They're, We're, Tom's, Jane's, etc.*

I'm in seventh heaven.

I'm walking on air.

I'm on top of the world.

I'm sitting on top of the world.

I'm high on life.

I'm feeling good.

I'm feeling fine.

I'm as merry as the day is long.

I'm happy as can be.

I'm happy as a clam.

I'm as happy as a clam.

I'm as pleased as punch.

I'm beside myself with joy.

I couldn't be happier.

280   Expressing enthusiasm for life

Things couldn't be better.

Everything's coming up roses.

I don't have a care in the world.

What a great day!

It's great to be alive!

It feels good just to be alive!

Life's been good to me.

281   When someone is content

My mind's at ease.

I'm content.

We're satisfied.

I'm just going with the flow.

He's as snug as a bug in a rug.

I'm at peace. (*formal*)

282   When someone is carefree

I'm footloose and fancy-free. (*cliché*)

I don't have a care in the world.

Tom is without a care in the world.

I haven't a care.

283   When someone is resigned to life as it is

I accept myself for what I am.

I've come to terms with myself.

I've come to terms with reality.

I've come to grips with reality.

I've learned to face the music. (*idiomatic*)

   to face the music = to face life; to face reality

Leave well enough alone. (*cliché*)

Let well enough alone.

Let sleeping dogs lie. (*cliché*)

> = *Do not try to solve a problem that is not causing extreme difficulties at the moment.*

284 Expressing displeasure with something

That leaves a lot to be desired.

That's not what I had in mind.

That didn't fit the bill.

> *to fit the bill = to be what is needed*

That doesn't quite suit me.

It's not up to snuff.

> *up to snuff = up to standard*

That's not what it's cracked up to be.

> *cracked up to be = said to be*

285 Asking someone to stop being unpleasant

Stop griping.

Stop complaining.

Quit complaining.

Quit whining.

Quit your bitching. (*mildly vulgar*)

Quit your kvetching. (*informal*)

> *kvetching = complaining*

Quit your beefing. (*slang*)

> *to beef = to complain*

Quit your bellyaching. (*slang*)

> *to bellyache = to complain*

Don't be such a grouch.

Don't be such a crab.

> *a crab = a crabby person = a grouchy person*

Don't be so grouchy.

Don't be so grumpy.

> *grumpy = irritable; out of sorts*

Did you get up on the wrong side of the bed? (*idiomatic*)

Somebody didn't get enough sleep.
Stop sulking.
Stop pouting.

286 Dullness and boredom

I'm bored.
I'm bored to tears.
I'm bored to death.
I'm bored to distraction.
I'm bored stiff.
I'm bored silly.
Ho-hum.
Are we having fun yet?
When does the fun start?
That went over like a lead balloon. (*idiomatic*)
That was a flop.

> *a flop = a failure*

That flopped.
What a yawner.

> *a yawner = something boring that causes yawns*

This is as dull as dishwater. (*cliché*)
He could go on forever.
He's like a broken record.
She really wears on me.
Wake me up when it's over.
I'm sick and tired of this.
I'm fed up.
I need a change of scenery.
I need a change of pace.

287 Dullness in people

Must you harp on the same string?
Must you keep harping on that?
Must you dwell on the subject?

Must you beat a dead horse?

Don't be such a stick-in-the-mud.

Don't be such a party pooper. (*jocular*)

> *a party pooper = a dull person who ruins parties*

Don't be such a wet blanket. (*informal*)

> *a wet blanket = someone who ruins all the fun, as a wet blanket smothers a fire*

Don't be such a killjoy. (*informal*)

> *a killjoy = someone who ruins all the fun*

288 Excitement in people

She's the life of the party.

He's (such) a card.

He's a kill. (*slang*)

ANXIETY

289 When you feel out of place

I was in the wrong place at the wrong time.

I feel like a fish out of water.

I'm out of my element.

When in Rome, do as the Romans do. (*cliché*)

When in Rome. (*informal*)

290 Expressing anger

I'm so furious.

I'm so mad I could scream.

I've never been so mad in my life.

I was chewing nails.

Tom was loaded for bear.

If looks could kill . . .

291 Expressing fright

I was scared.

I was frightened.

I was terrified.

I was petrified.

I was scared to death.

I was scared silly.

You scared me.

You frightened me.

You scared the hell out of me. (*mildly vulgar*)

You scared the crap out of me. (*mildly vulgar*)

You scared the dickens out of me.

You scared the devil out of me.

You scared the wits out of me.

You scared me out of my wits.

You scared me to death.

You scared the daylights out of me.

You scared the living daylights out of me.

You scared the pants off me. (*informal*)

I almost jumped out of my skin.

I almost lost it.

It gave me the creeps. (*slang*)

It gave me the willies. (*slang*)

It made my flesh crawl.

It gave me goose bumps.

It gave me goose pimples.

It curled my hair.

My hair stood on end.

My blood ran cold.

My blood curdled.

It set my teeth on edge.

292   When you do not know what to say

I'm at a loss for words.

I'm speechless.

I'm dumbstruck.

No comment.

I have no response.

I have nothing to say.

I have nothing to add.

I don't know what to say.

What can I say?

What do you want me to say?

You got me there.

THE SENSES

293 **Difficulty in hearing**

I'm sorry, I'm hard of hearing.

I'm sorry, I'm hearing-impaired.

He suffered a hearing loss.

He's stone deaf.

> *stone = completely*

She's deaf as a post. (*informal*)

294 **Lacking an ear for music**

I don't have an ear for music.

I'm tone-deaf.

He's got an ear for the piano.

She plays piano by ear.

295 **Hearing loud and soft sounds**

I can't hear them; they're out of earshot.

It was so quiet you could hear a pin drop.

That noise is deafening.

That noise assaults the ear. (*formal*)

That noise is setting my teeth on edge.

What a racket!

> *racket = noise*

Are you trying to wake the dead?

My ears are ringing.

296   Concerning ears or hearing

My plea fell on deaf ears. (*cliché*)

They turned a deaf ear to our plea. (*idiomatic*)

There's none so deaf as those who will not hear. (*cliché*)

In one ear and out the other. (*cliché*)

To hear tell, the whole situation was awful.

Boy, did I get an earful.

   an earful = a long explanation; a scolding

Prick up your ears! (*idiomatic*)

Keep your ears open.

Hear no evil. (*cliché*)

297   The taste of foods

Delicious.

That tastes great.

Tastes great.

That's as sweet as honey.

That's as sweet as sugar.

That tastes terrible.

That tastes like chicken.

That turns my stomach.

That's unfit for human consumption.

298   Offering someone a small portion of food

Would you like a taste?

Here. Try some.

Would you like a sip?

299   Expressing hunger

I'm hungry.

I'm famished.

I'm starved.

I'm ravenous.

My mouth is watering.

That stew is mouth-watering.

I'm so hungry I could eat a horse. (*cliché*)

I could eat a horse. (*cliché*)

300   Identifying smells

What's that smell?

What smells?

Do you smell something?

What's that fragrance?

What's that aroma?

What's that scent?

What's that odor?

What's that stench?

What stinks? (*informal*)

Do you smell gas?

Get a whiff of this!

Take a whiff of this.

Sniff this.

That smells.

That smells to high heaven!

That stinks to high heaven! (*informal*)

It stinks on ice. (*slang*)

301   Physical responses

That sends shivers down my spine.

It gave me goose bumps.

It gave me the chills.

It gave me butterflies in my stomach. (*idiomatic*)

302   The sense of touch

It was (as) soft as silk.

It was (as) hard as a rock.

It was (as) hard as stone.

The fish felt slimy.

303 Difficulties with seeing

I'm as blind as a bat. (*cliché*)

I can't see a thing without my glasses.

I can't quite make it out.

304 Concerning good vision

I have good eyesight.

I have excellent vision.

I have 20/20 vision.

I've got a good eye for color.

I've got an eye for composition.

305 Concerning vision and belief

I can't believe my eyes.

My eyes betray me. (*formal*)

Do my eyes deceive me?

There's none so blind as those who will not see. (*cliché*)

LOVE AND SEX

306 Asking someone for a date

Are you free Saturday evening?

Are you free Saturday night?

Are you busy on the 15th?

What are you up to this weekend?

What are you doing next weekend?

Would you like to go to dinner?

Would you like to go out to dinner with me?

I was wondering if you'd like to go out.

I was wondering if you'd like to see a movie.

If you're not doing anything, would you like to go to a
party with me?

If you don't have other plans, would you like to go
dancing?

307 Concerning romantic or sexual attraction

He's really cute.

She's really attractive.

He's really my type.

She's really a doll. (*informal*)

He's a real doll. (*informal*)

She's a real babe. (*informal*)

He's a real looker. (*informal*)

She's really gorgeous.

He's really handsome.

He's really a stud. (*slang*)

He's really a hunk. (*slang*)

She's really pretty.

She's really lovely.

She's really beautiful.

What a stud. (*slang, male only*)

What a hunk. (*slang, male only*)

What a babe.

What a doll.

What a (good-)looker.

What a loser.

What a slut. (*rude, female only*)

What a bimbo. (*slang, female only*)

What a geek. (*slang, usually male*)

308 Professing love

I love you.

I really love you.

I'm falling in love with you.

I've fallen in love with you.

I'm in love with you.

I'm madly in love with you.

I'm passionately in love with you.

I'm madly, passionately in love with you.

I love you madly.

I love you passionately.

I love you with all my heart.

I've never loved anyone like this before.

I adore you.

I worship you.

I want you.

I need you.

I have to have you.

I've got to have you.

I'm yours.

Take me; I'm yours.

Be mine.

Be mine always.

Be my love.

Be my sweetheart.

Be my valentine.

> *a valentine = a special person on St. Valentine's day*

309 Describing your love or lover

She's my true love.

He's my one and only.

She's the love of my life.

I'm in love.

I'm falling in love.

I've fallen in love.

I'm head over heels in love.

I'm madly in love.

I'm passionately in love.

My head is in a cloud.

I'm walking on air.

310 Concerning pregnancy

She's pregnant.

They're expecting.

She's with child. (*formal*)

She's in a family way.

There's a bun in the oven. (*slang*)

She's baking bread. (*euphemistic*)

She got knocked up. (*mildly vulgar*)

He knocked her up. (*mildly vulgar*)

Are you expecting (a child)?

When are you due?

It's due in March.

Who's the father?

Do you have any names picked out?

Are you hoping for a boy or a girl?

Do you know if it's a boy or a girl?

I'm so happy for you!

311 Sexual expressions

I'm in the mood.

I'm all hot to trot. (*slang*)

> = *I am sexually aroused or interested.*

I'm really horny. (*vulgar*)

> *horny = sexually aroused*

I'm horny as hell. (*vulgar*)

Did you do it?

> *to do it = to copulate*

Did you sleep together?

> *to sleep together = to copulate*

Did you make it?

> *to make it = to copulate*

Did you go all the way?

> *to go all the way = to copulate*

Did you screw? (*vulgar*)

> *to screw = to copulate*

Did you get any action? (*vulgar*)

    action = sex

Did you score?

    score = copulate

It was a one-night stand.

    one-night stand = a single night of copulation

It was just a one-nighter.

No strings attached.

I only got to first base.

We didn't go all the way.

We went all the way.

I scored.

We had sex.

We made love.

We consummated our relationship. (*formal*)

We had sexual intercourse. (*formal*)

We had intercourse. (*formal*)

I knew her in the biblical sense. (*formal*)

If you can't be good, be careful.

312   Sexually phrased insults and retorts

Don't jerk me off. (*slang*)

Don't jerk me around. (*slang*)

Don't pull my chain. (*slang*)

Stop pulling my chain. (*slang*)

Stop jerking me off. (*slang*)

Bugger off. (*slang*)

Screw you. (*taboo*)

313   Turning someone down

I'm not interested.

I'm seeing someone else.

I have other plans.

Something suddenly came up.

I have to wash my hair.

My calendar is full.

You're not my type.

Not if you were the last man on earth. (*rude*)

You must be joking. (*rude*)

I don't feel up to it.

I have a headache.

Please. (*with a disgusted tone of voice*)

FAMILY
MATTERS

HOMELIFE

314 Describing family relationships

You're just like your mother.

You take after your father.

You are your father all over again.

It's like I'm talking to your mother.

She looks just like her mother.

She looks just like her mother did at that age.

She's the picture of her mother.

She favors her mother.

He's the spit and image of his grandfather.

He's the spitting image of his grandfather.

He's got his father's features.

She's got her mother's nose.

    = *Her nose is very much like her mother's nose.*

She resembles her Aunt Martha.

He's a chip off the old block.

She's following in her father's footsteps.

Like father, like son.

Like mother, like daughter.

He's a real mama's boy.

She's a real daddy's girl.

She's daddy's little girl.

315 Family solidarity

We are (all) family.

Blood runs thicker than water.

How can you do that to your own flesh and blood?

The family that prays together stays together. (*cliché*)

316 Asking about a meal

When do we eat?

What's to eat?

What's for supper?

What are we having?

317 Announcing a meal

Dinner's almost ready.

It's almost done.

It will be on the table in a minute.

It's almost ready.

(It's) time to eat.

Dinner's ready.

Soup's on! (*informal*)

    = *Dinner's ready!*

318 Instructions given to children in the kitchen

Don't sit on the counter.

Don't eat that; you'll spoil your dinner.

Don't stand in front of the refrigerator with the door open.

Watch out; it's hot!

Don't drink milk out of the carton!

Don't drink milk out of the jug!

Would you set the table?

Go sit down; supper's ready.

Go tell your father supper's ready.

Call the family to dinner.

Call everyone to the table.

319 Blessing the food

Sarah, would you say grace?

Who wants to say grace?

Fold your hands.

320   Second servings

Could you pour me some more milk?

More milk please.

Could I have seconds, please?

May I have seconds, please?

Would you like some more of this?

Is there any more of this?

What's for dessert?

321   Instructing children on good table manners

Don't put your elbows on the table.

Don't talk with your mouth full.

Don't read at the table.

No TV during dinner.

TV = television

Wipe your mouth.

Put your napkin on your lap.

Put your napkin in your lap.

322   Doing the dishes

Andrew, please clear the table.

Please put your dishes in the sink.

dishes = all crockery and utensils

Please carry your own dishes to the kitchen.

It's your turn to do the dishes.

It's your turn to clear the table.

I'll scrape and you load (the dishwasher).

Whose turn is it to do the dishes?

I'll wash and you dry.

323   Asking to leave the dinner table early

May I please leave the table?

(said by a child)

May I be excused?
> *(said by a child)*

Do you mind if I leave the table?
> *(said by an adult)*

I'll have to excuse myself.
> *(said by an adult)*

Would you excuse me?

324   Instructing children to finish eating

Finish your dinner.

You have to eat everything.

You have to eat everything that you serve yourself.

You have to eat some of everything.

You have to clean up your plate.

If you don't eat your vegetables, you won't get any dessert.

If you don't eat your dinner, you won't get any dessert.

There are starving children in Africa.
> *Africa ≈ Bosnia, Asia, South America, etc.*

325   Concerning a radio or stereo

Turn the stereo down.

Turn the stereo off.

Turn the radio off.

Let's find a different station.

What station is this?

What do you want to hear?

326   Concerning furniture or carpeting

Don't wear your shoes on the good carpet.

Don't sit on the good furniture.

Don't put your feet on the furniture.

Keep your feet off (of) the furniture.

327   Concerning television

What's on TV?

> *TV = television*

What's on?

What's on tonight?

What's on the tube?

> *the tube = the television (picture tube)*

What's on channel five?

What do you want to watch?

What do you want to see?

What are you watching?

Where is the TV guide?

Where is the TV listing?

Is this any good?

Is there anything on?

There anything good on?

328   Changing the television channel

Find a channel and stick with it. (*informal*)

Stick with one channel. (*informal*)

Stick to one channel. (*informal*)

Stop flipping channels. (*informal*)

Change the channel.

Let's change the channel.

Hand me the remote control.

Where is the remote (control)?

Give me the remote.

329   Managing a television set

You're sitting too close to the TV.

Can't you get a better picture?

Turn the TV off if you're not watching it.

Turn it up, please.

Please adjust the rabbit ears.

> *rabbit ears = a type of indoor television antenna*

Please adjust the antenna.

Turn it down.

Could you please turn it down?

Please turn down the TV.

Turn it off.

330 Taking a nap

I'm going to take a nap.

I'm going to take a catnap.

> *a catnap = a short nap*

I'm going to take a snooze.

> *a snooze = a nap*

I'm going to get some shut-eye.

> *some shut-eye = some sleep*

I'm going to catch forty winks.

> *forty winks = some sleep*

I'm going to catch some Z's.

> *Z's = snoring = sleep*

331 Going to bed and to sleep

I'm off to bed.

I'm going to bed.

It's bedtime.

It's past my bedtime.

I'm going to sleep.

I'm going to hit the sack. (*idiomatic*)

I'm going to hit the hay. (*idiomatic*)

I'm going to crash. (*slang*)

I think I'll retire for the night. (*formal*)

I think I'll say good night now.

332 Saying good night

Good night.

Sleep tight. Don't let the bedbugs bite.

(usually said to a child)

See you in the morning.

Sweet dreams.

Pleasant dreams.

Sleep well.

Night-night.

(usually said to a child)

Nighty-night.

(usually said to a child)

333 Commands for a dog

Sit.

Stay.

Roll over.

Shake hands.

Shake.

Play dead.

Fetch!

Heel.

Sic 'em.

sic = attack

Come!

Come here.

Here, boy!

Here, girl!

Good boy!

Good girl!

Bad dog!

Do you want to go outside?

334   Caring for pets

Did you walk the dog?

Someone has to walk the dog.

Will you please put the cat out?

The dog wants to get out.

Where is the gerbil?

The guinea pig is loose again.

Please clean the (cat's) litter (box) now!

The cat's litter needs changing.

We're out of dog chow.

dog chow = dried dog food

EDUCATION

335   Getting ready to study or do homework

Time to crack the books.

to crack = to open

Time to hit the books.

to hit = to use

Gotta cram. (*slang*)

to cram = to study hard; to cram knowledge into one's brain

I need to cram for a final. (*slang*)

I have a lot of studying to do.

I have to study.

I've got to study.

I've got a midterm tomorrow.

I've got a final exam tomorrow.

I've got a big test tomorrow.

I've got a big exam tomorrow.

336   Talking to a child's teacher

I'd like to discuss my daughter's progress.

I'd like to talk about my daughter's grade.

How is my daughter doing in class?

My daughter seems to be having trouble in class.

She's having a hard time with her homework.

What can I do to help her at home?

How can I help her with her homework?

337 Returning to school after an absence

Do you have a note from home?

Do you have a note from your mother?

Do you have a note from your doctor?

338 Questioning a college professor

Can I still get into your course?

What texts are required?

What is the book list for the course?

Is a paper required for this course?

Is there a final for this course?

Is attendance required in this course?

What are the requirements?

When are your office hours?

Where is your office?

339 Asking for clarification in a college classroom

Could you explain that again?

I don't get it. Please explain.

Please go over that part again.

I don't understand.

I still don't understand.

I do not understand your English. Please speak more plainly.

I'm having a problem understanding the TA.

TA = Teaching Assistant

340 Asking about classroom examinations
When is the final (exam)?
When is the midterm?
What do you want us to know for the test?
What will the test cover?
Will there be a review session?
Will the test cover the whole book?
Will the test take the whole period?
What's on the test?

341 Asking about a classroom assignment
How many pages do we have to read for Monday?
How many pages?
Will we have to turn in our homework?
What's the reading assignment for next time?
Will there be a quiz?
What's the assignment for tomorrow?

342 Asking about grades
Can you tell me what grade I'm getting?
Would you tell me what grade I'm getting?
Do you grade on a curve?
How many A's were there?
What's the grading curve?
I worked hard, so don't I deserve a good grade?
Can I talk to you about my grade?

CHILDREN

343 Expressions used in children's games
You're it!
Not it!
Olly olly oxen free.
Last one there's a rotten egg.

Step on a crack; break your mother's back.

Finders keepers, losers weepers.

344   Claiming the rights to something

I got dibs on the apple pie!

dibs = a claim

Dibs on the apple pie!

Dibsies!

345   When children bicker

You got cooties! (*informal*)

cooties = lice

Stop making fun of me.

Stop picking on me.

Leave me alone.

I'm telling Mom.

I'm going to tell on you.

I'm telling.

Sticks and stones may break my bones, but names will
   never hurt me.

I'm rubber and you're glue; whatever you say bounces off
   me and sticks to you.

I know you are, but what am I?

Meanie!

346   Meeting children

And how are you today?

And what is your name?

How old are you?

347   Concerning a child's growth and development

You've gotten so big!

You're growing so tall.

Your turning into (quite) a little lady.

Your turning into (quite) a little gentleman.
What a big girl!
My, my! Haven't you grown!

348 **Posing questions to children**
What grade are you in?
How do you like school?
Do you go to school yet?
How many years till you're in school?
What's your favorite subject in school?
Have you been a good boy?
Are you being a good girl?
How many brothers and sisters do you have?

349 **Praising a small child**
That's very good.
You're a good little boy.
You're a good little girl.
Good boy!
Good girl!
Big boy!
What a big girl!
I'm so proud of you.
Mommy's proud of you.
We are very proud of you.

350 **Scolding a child**
Behave.
Behave yourself.
Be good.
Be a good girl.
Be a good boy.
That's enough of that!

351 Encouraging a child to be quiet
Sit down.
Be quiet.
Quiet!
Let's be quiet.
Shhh!
Hush!
Not another word!
I don't want to hear a(nother) peep out of you!
  a peep = a sound
I don't want to hear a single peep out of you!

352 Asking a child to stop some behavior
Stop it.
Stop that.
Settle down.
That's enough of that!
Simmer down.

353 Asking a child to leave things alone
Put that down.
Keep your hands to yourself.
Look with your eyes not your hands. (*cliché*)
Put that away.
Leave that alone.
Don't touch that.

354 Asking a child to leave people alone
Don't bother your father while he's driving.
Stop pestering your little brother.
Keep your hands to yourself.
Keep your hands off your little brother.
Stop teasing your little sister.

Leave him alone.

Leave him be.

Let him be.

355   Giving a child instructions for cleanliness or tidiness

Clean up your room.

Pick up your room.

Pick up your clothes.

Put your toys away.

Make your bed.

Go wash your hands.

Go wash your face.

Go brush your teeth.

Comb your hair.

Be sure and wash behind your ears.

356   Instructing a child in good posture

Sit up straight.

Don't slouch (down) (in your chair).

Stand up straight.

Don't walk all bent over.

Stand tall.

357   Giving a child instructions at dinner time

Keep your mouth closed.

Chew with your mouth closed.

Don't talk with your mouth full.

Close your mouth while you're eating.

Put your napkin in your lap.

Get your elbows off the table.

Don't wolf your food down like that.

You'll get a stomachache.

Eat your vegetables.

Eat all your vegetables.

Finish your vegetables.

No dessert until you finish your vegetables.

No dessert unless you clean (up) your plate.

No dessert unless you finish your dinner.

358   Giving a child instructions for television watching

Move back from the TV.

Turn that thing off.

Turn that music down.

Turn that racket down.

    racket = noise

I can't hear myself think with all that racket.

359   Instructing a child in personal safety

Don't talk to strangers.

Don't take food or candy from somebody you don't know.

Never get into a car with a stranger.

Don't play with that. You'll put your eye(s) out.

Look before you leap. (*cliché*)

Look both ways (before crossing the street).

Keep both hands on the handlebars.

You're going to break your neck.

If you make that face again, your face will freeze that
    way.

360   Concerning a child's homework

Do your homework.

Did you finish your homework?

You can't go outside until you finish your homework.

You can't watch television until you finish your
    homework.

No television until you finish your homework.

Can I help you with your homework?

Don't forget to take your homework to school.

Do you have any homework tonight?

Let's see your homework.

361   Sending a child to bed

It's time to go to bed.

Off to bed now.

Go to bed.

It's bedtime.

It's past your bedtime.

362   When a parent is frustrated with a child's behavior

I told you to go before we left.

How many times have I told you to stop that?

How many times do I have to tell you?

If I've told you once, I've told you a thousand times.

Why can't you behave?

When will you learn?

I've had it up to here with you.

Listen to me when I'm talking to you.

I'll give you what for.

Because I said so.

Because.

Do you want a spanking?

Do you want a time-out?

Do you want to be grounded?

Go to your room.

I want you to go to your room and think about what you did.

You're grounded.

I'm grounding you.

363   Making sure a child understands

Do as I say.

Do as I say, not as I do.

Do as I tell you.

Do what I tell you.

Do as you're told.

Do you understand?

Understand?

Is that clear?

Have I made myself clear?

Do I make myself clear?

Do I make myself perfectly clear?

Did you hear me?

Do you hear me?

Do you hear?

364 Concerning a child's use of good manners

Mind your manners.

Mind your Ps and Qs. (*idiomatic*)

Behave.

Behave yourself.

I expect you to be on your best behavior.

Act like a lady.

Act like a gentleman.

Say "excuse me."

Say "thank you."

Say "you're welcome."

Say "please."

What's the magic word?

　　the magic word = *the word* please

What do you say?

　　= *Say "please."*

Yes, what?

　　= *Say "Yes, sir; Yes, ma'am; or Yes, please."*

(Always) remember to say please and thank you.

MONEY MATTERS

BANKING

365   A bank teller greeting a patron

How can I help you?

Can I help you with something?

How may I help you? (*formal*)

I'm open over here.

I'm open down here.

> *down here = over here*

I can help you down here.

Please step down.

Next.

Next, please.

Yes? (*informal*)

366   Basic requests to a bank teller

I'd like to cash a check.

> *I'd like to ≈ I need to, I want to, Can I please (?),*
> *Can I (?)*

I'd like to cash these traveler's checks.

I'd like to cash (in) these savings bonds.

I'd like to make a deposit.

I'd like to transfer money into my savings account.

I'd like to withdraw money from my account.

I'd like to make a withdrawal.

367   Requesting large or small bills when cashing a check

Tens and twenties, please.

Large bills, please.

It doesn't matter (which denominations).

Give me all twenties.

No small bills.

368 Requesting change from a teller or cashier

I need (some) change.

I need ≈ Could I please have (?), I'd like, Please give me, Let me have

I need some change, please.

I need a roll of quarters.

Gimme some change. (*informal*)

How 'bout some change? (*informal*)

369 General banking matters

Out-of-state checks will take one week to clear.

Are you a customer here?

May I see some identification?

I need to see some identification.

May I see some ID?

ID = identification

Do you have any ID?

Do you have your bank ID card?

Enter your personal identification number here.

Press your PIN number here.

PIN = personal identification number

Is your name on the account?

Endorse this, please.

to endorse = to sign on the back

Initial this, please.

Let me check with my supervisor.

You are overdrawn.

You will have to speak to a bank officer (about that).

370   Using the automatic (mechanical) teller

Where is the automatic teller machine?

> *Where is the* ≈ *Do you have a, Where would I find the, Where's the*

The ATM kept my card.

> *ATM = automatic teller machine*

The ATM won't give me my card back.

The ATM ate my card. (*informal*)

371   Basic requests to a personal banker

I'd like to open a savings account.

> *I'd like to* ≈ *I need to, I want to, Can I (?)*

I'd like to close out my savings account.

I'd like to open a checking account.

I'd like to close my checking account.

I'd like to close my account.

I'd like to get a safety deposit box.

I'd like to apply for a loan.

I'd like to purchase a certificate of deposit.

I'd like to buy a CD.

> *CD = certificate of deposit*

372   Concerning a bank account

What's the interest rate?

I believe that there is an error in my account.

I need to order new checks.

I want to order some new checks.

Can I order new checks?

Please explain the service charges on this account.

Is this account insured by the federal government?

Do you have bank by mail?

> *bank by mail = bank deposits by mail*

Can you give me a new banking card?

373 Asking about foreign exchange

Do you handle foreign exchange here?
Does this bank handle foreign exchange?
I'd like to change some foreign currency.
I'd like to buy some foreign currency.
What's the current exchange rate?
We don't handle foreign exchange here.

374 Information about foreign exchange rates

What is the exchange rate of marks to the dollar?

> *marks ≈ yen, lira, pesetas, pesos, francs, etc.*

The exchange rate is 1.5 marks to the dollar.
The exchange rate is going up.
How many pounds to the dollar?
How many francs to the dollar?

375 Banking hours

When are you open?
When do you open?
How late are you open (today)?
What are your hours?
Are you open on weekends?
Are you open on Saturday?
Are you open after five?
What are the hours for the bank vault?

376 A teller inquiring about the size of bills that you want

How would you like that?
Large or small bills?
Any preference?

377 Requesting a loan from a banker

I'd like to apply for a loan.

I'd like to apply for a mortgage.

I'd like to apply for a home equity loan.

I need to mortgage my home.

I need a second mortgage.

I'd like a self-amortizing loan term.

I'd like a variable interest rate mortgage.

I'd like an adjustable rate mortgage.

378   Asking about loans at a bank

Please explain a balloon loan.

> *Please explain ≈ Can you tell me something about (?),
> Tell me more about, I don't understand*

Please explain an adjustable rate mortgage.

Please explain an ARM.

> *ARM = adjustable rate mortgage*

Please explain a fixed rate loan.

What is your best interest rate?

Do you have any 30-year terms available?

Do you provide balloon loans?

> *balloon loan = a loan where the balance must be paid
> in full after a few years*

Do you offer balloon loans?

What are my monthly principal and interest payments?

How much are my monthly principal and interest
payments?

What is the monthly tax and insurance escrow amount?

> *escrow = money deposited for later use*

Is there a prepayment penalty?

What are the closing costs?

> *closing costs = the costs of mortgaging a house*

What are the closing requirements?

How large a down payment is required?

What is the total out-of-pocket cost required at closing?

> *out-of-pocket cost = money that must be paid in cash
> at a particular time*

PERSONAL FINANCES

379 Controlling expenses

We have to watch our spending.

We need to watch our money.

We need to watch our pennies.

We've got to watch every dime.

We have to control our spending.

We have to keep track of our expenses more closely.

We have to cut back on expenses.

We've got to start budgeting our money.

We've got to tighten our belt.

We've got to save our pennies.

We must cut the frills.

> *frills = unnecessary expenditures*

We'll have to go back to the basics.

We have to trim the budget.

> *trim = reduce*

I'm on a strict budget.

I can't afford that.

I don't have the cash for it.

I'm in the red.

I'm robbing Peter to pay Paul. (*cliché*)

380 Spending a lot of money

I'll dip into my savings.

I'll scrounge up the money somehow.

> *scrounge = locate with difficulty*

I'll get it somehow.

I've got enough saved up.

I've been saving for a rainy day. (*cliché*)

I've been saving my pennies.

I've been saving up for this.

How much is this going to set me back?

> *to set me back = to cost me*

Do you have any financing plans?

Can I pay in installments?

381 Attitudes toward spending money

What a miser! (*informal*)

What a tightwad. (*informal*)

   a tightwad = a miserly person

Don't spend it all in one place. (*cliché*)

   = Don't be foolish with your money.

Don't let it burn a hole in your pocket. (*idiomatic*)

   = Try to keep your money from finding a way out of your pocket.

You spend money as if it were going out of style.

You have no business throwing money around like that.

You might as well flush it down the toilet. (*informal*)

You're living beyond your means.

That cost a pretty penny. (*idiomatic*)

   a pretty penny = a large sum of money

That cost an arm and a leg. (*idiomatic*)

   an arm and a leg = a great deal of money

Money is no object.

382 Attitudes toward spending money — clichés

A penny saved is a penny earned.

Penny wise, pound foolish.

You can't take it with you.

Money doesn't grow on trees.

A fool and his money are soon parted.

He's laughing all the way to the bank.

(The love of) money is the root of all evil.

FOOD AND DRINK

SUPERMARKETS

383 **Locating things in a supermarket**

Where will I find the ketchup?

Do you carry diet root beer?

What aisle is the canned salmon in?

In what aisle is the frozen food?

Can you tell me where I can find chocolate milk?

Where is the chocolate milk?

384 **When supplies run out at a grocery store**

I'm afraid we're out of that item.

I'm afraid we don't carry that.

I'm afraid we don't have it in stock.

Would you like a rain check?

> *a rain check = a certificate that allows you to purchase an out-of-stock sale item at a sale price after the sale has expired*

385 **Asking about payment at a grocery store**

Do you take checks?

Can I make this out over the amount of purchase?

Can I make this out for more than the amount of purchase?

Can I make this out for more?

386 **Requesting instructions for packing your purchases**

Do you want paper or plastic bags?

Paper or plastic?

Do you want to carry the greeting card separately?

Do you want the milk bagged?

Do you want your receipt in the bag?

387 Making special requests to a bag packer at a grocery store

I'd like paper bags.

Paper bags, please.

Paper.

I'd like plastic bags.

Plastic bags, please.

Plastic.

Don't crush the bread.

    bread ≈ *eggs, potato chips, flowers, etc.*

Don't mash the bread.

388 Asking about sales and money-off coupons

Any coupons?

Do you have any coupons?

Hasn't this coupon expired?

The sale doesn't start until tomorrow.

That item is no longer on sale.

This goes on sale tomorrow.

I have some coupons.

I have coupons.

Here are my coupons.

Do you take food stamps?

This item was marked on sale.

How long is this on sale?

389 A clerk asking about prices

Can you give me a price check?

Do you remember how much this cost?

Do you know how much this was?

Do you remember which aisle this was in?

390   A clerk asking about payment

Do you have a check-cashing card?

How will you pay for this?

Cash or charge?

Will you be using a credit card?

Do you have any small change?

391   Asking for change at a grocery store

Can I have change for a twenty?

Can I have telephone change, please?

> *telephone change = coins that can be used in a pay
> telephone*

Could I have some quarters, please?

Could you give me the change in quarters?

392   Buying beverage alcohol at a supermarket

May I see your ID?

> *ID = identification*

May I see some ID?

I need to see some identification.

I need to see some ID.

Can I see your driver's license?

Do you have ID?

Do you have (any) identification?

May I see proof of your age? (*formal*)

**393   Asking questions at the grocery store service
counter**

Can I cash a check?

Can I rent a carpet cleaner?

Do you sell (postage) stamps here?

Can I buy a money order here?

Is this where I drop off film to be developed?

Is this where I drop off film to be processed?

Are my photos developed yet?

394   Getting grocery store purchases to the car

Do you need a pickup?

> *a pickup = a ticket to use in retrieving your groceries,
> which will be guarded while you fetch your car*

Do you need a carryout?

> *a carryout = some help carrying the bags to the car*

Do you need help with that?

FAST FOOD

395   A fast-food clerk taking an order

Can I take your order?

May I take your order, please?

What would you like?

May I help you?

Can I help you?

What will it be?

What'll it be?

Small, medium, or large?

**396   A fast-food clerk asking where the food will be
eaten**

For here or to go?

> *to go = packaged to be taken out and eaten elsewhere*

Will this be for here or to go?

Do you want that to go?

Is that for here or to go?

Are you going to eat it here?

397   Placing an order for fast-food products

(Give me) a burger and fries.

> *Give me ≈ I'd like, I'll take, I'll have, Please give me,
> Gimme, Let's have, I need*

(Give me) a burger with everything.

> *a burger = a hamburger sandwich*

(Give me) a cheeseburger and fries.

a cheeseburger = a hamburger with cheese on the meat pattie

(Give me) a hot dog with the works, please.

a hot dog = a frankfurter or wiener sandwich, using a specially shaped bun

(Give me) a dog with the works.

a dog = a hot dog

(Give me) an order of fries.

fries = deep-fried potato sticks

(Give me) a shake.

a shake = a milk shake, chocolate unless another flavor is specified

(Give me) a cheeseburger, large fries, and a shake.

large fries = a large order of fries

(Give me) a cheeseburger, large fry, and a cola.

fry = an order of deep-fried potato sticks

(Give me) a small soda.

a soda = a carbonated drink

(Give me) a Coke.

a Coke = a serving of Coca-Cola brand carbonated beverage

(Give me) a Pepsi.

a Pepsi = a serving of Pepsi brand carbonated beverage

(Give me) a small soda, no ice.

(Give me) a large fry.

(Give me) cheese with that.

(Give me) extra mustard.

(Give me) ketchup for the fries.

No ice, please.

(I'll have) one salad bar and an iced tea.

one salad bar = the right for one person to select a meal from the do-it-yourself salad selections

398   **Ordering drinks at a fast-food restaurant**
What kind of drinks do you have?
What kind of drinks you got? (*informal*)
What do you have to drink?
Got any pepper? (*informal*)
(I) need some salt.
Where are the napkins?
Where are the straws?

> *straws = paper or plastic drinking straws*

Can I have some napkins?

399   **Special instructions for a fast-food clerk**
No ketchup.
No onions.
Hold the onions.
Hold the mayo.

> *mayo = mayonnaise*

Go easy on the onions.
Take it easy on the onions.
Take it easy with the onions.

400   **Telling where a fast-food order will be eaten**
To go, please.

> *to go = packaged to be taken out and eaten elsewhere*

I need that to go, please.
For here, please.
I'll eat it here.

401   **A fast-food clerk offering food items**
What would you like on your hot dog?
(Do) you want that with everything?

> *everything = onions, pickles, hot peppers, mustard,*
> *ketchup, and possibly tomato, lettuce, and mayonnaise*

Can I get you something to drink with that?

What do you want to drink?

What about something to drink?

Would you like fries with that?

What size?

Will that be a large soft drink?

Would you like some salt and pepper?

The mustard and ketchup are over there.

Do you need any ketchup?

Do you need any napkins?

402   A fast-food clerk delivering an order

Here you go.

There you go.

Here is your order.

Here's your change.

Thank you and come again.

403   Complaining about a fast-food order

This isn't what I ordered.

This burger is cold.

Where's my large drink?

You completely messed up my order! (*informal*)

I didn't order this burger!

These fries are too greasy.

Look, this meat is still pink!

CAFÉS AND SANDWICH SHOPS

404   Taking your order

Can I take your order?

What would you like?

Can I help you?

What will it be?

What'll it be?

405 Placing an order in a café

I'd like a (ham)burger and (French) fries.

> *I'd like* ≈ *Give me, I'll take, I'll have, Please give me, Gimme, Let's have*

I'll have a burger with everything.

> *a burger = a hamburger sandwich*

I'll have a cheeseburger and fries.

> *a cheeseburger = a hamburger with cheese on the meat pattie*

I'll have an order of fries.

> *fries = deep-fried potato sticks*

I'll have a cheeseburger, large fries, and a shake.

> *large fries = a large order of fries*

I'll have the roast beef special.

What about a small sub?

> *a sub = a submarine sandwich = a sandwich with many ingredients on a long bun*

A large bowl of chili, please.

Do you have any vegetable soup?

What about liver and onions?

406 Special instructions at a café

No ketchup.

No onions.

Hold the onions.

Hold the mayo.

> *mayo = mayonnaise*

Go easy on the onions.

Take it easy on the onions.

Take it easy with the onions.

407 Ordering drinks at a café

What kind of drinks do you have?

What kind of drinks you got? (*informal*)

What do you have to drink?

I'll have a small soda.

> *a soda = a carbonated drink*

I'll have a Coke.

> *a Coke = a serving of Coca-Cola brand carbonated beverage*

I'll have a Pepsi.

> *a Pepsi = a serving of Pepsi brand carbonated beverage*

I'll have a small Coke, no ice.

PIZZA

408   Taking your order for a pizza

What'll it be?

Can I take your order?

What size?

What size would you like?

What size will that be?

Thick or thin crust?

Thick or thin?

What would you like on that?

Do you want any extras on that?

Would you like something to drink with that?

409   Placing a telephone order for pizza

I'll have a small pizza.

> *I'll have ≈ Please give me, Give me, I'll take, Make mine, I'd like to order, Gimme, Do you have (?), Let me have*

I'd like a medium pizza, please.

I'd like a large, please.

I'd like thin crust, please.

I'd like a vegetarian pizza.

I'd like pepperoni and mushrooms.

   pepperoni = a spicy Italian sausage (sliced very thin)

I'd like one medium cheese pizza, please.

I'd like a small thin crust, sausage and onion.

I'd like half cheese, half sausage.

I'd like just cheese.

I'd like a pizza with the works.

   the works = everything; all the different toppings

I'd like the works.

I'd like no anchovies.

I'd like everything but anchovies.

I'd like everything but onions.

What do you have to drink?

Do you have any specials?

When will that be ready?

I have a coupon.

How much will it be?

410   Concerning pizza delivery

Do you deliver?

We're at Second and Elm.

I'll leave the light on.

I'll leave the porch light on.

How long will it be?

411   Questions about delivering pizza

Would you like that delivered?

Is this for pickup or delivery?

Pickup or delivery?

Name?

How do you spell that?

How's that spelled?

Can you spell that, please?

Address?

Phone?

Please turn on a porch light.

Please leave the porch light on.

It will be there in 30 minutes.

412   Paying for pizza

Do you have any coupons?

Your total is $8.95.

Your order comes to $8.95.

That comes to $8.95.

That'll be $8.95.

That's $8.95.

RESTAURANTS

413   Asking for a table at a restaurant

A table for one.

A table for two.

Two, please.

I would like a nonsmoking table for two.

I have a reservation.

414   Concerning seating in a restaurant

Would you like smoking or nonsmoking?

Smoking or nonsmoking?

Smoking or non?

Do you have a reservation?

How many in your party?

Table for four?

Party of four?

party = group

Four?

We'll have a table ready in just a few minutes.

It'll be just a few minutes.

There's a ten-minute wait.

We have a table ready for Smith, party of four.

Table for Smith, party of four.

Smith, party of four.

Your waiter will be Alfredo.

Enjoy your meal. (*cliché*)

Enjoy. (*informal*)

415   Concerning smoking in a restaurant

Is this a nonsmoking restaurant?

Do you have a nonsmoking section?

I'd like the smoking section.

I'd like the nonsmoking section.

Please seat me as far as possible from the smoking
    section.

Smoking.

Nonsmoking.

**416   Explaining that someone else will join you at a
restaurant**

Another party will be sitting here.

We are waiting for another couple.

My friend will be along shortly.

I am expecting someone else.

I'm waiting for someone else.

417   Greetings from a waiter or waitress

Hello.

Sorry to keep you waiting.

How are you today?

My name's Sandy. I'll be your waitress this evening.

My name's Sandy. I'll be your server this evening.

I'm Bobby. I'm your server.

418   Questions a waiter or waitress might ask

Are you waiting for someone?

Will someone be joining you?

Good evening, would you care for a drink?

Would you like to start with a cocktail?

Would you like something to drink first?

Would you like to order a drink?

Can I get you something to drink?

Would anyone like coffee?

Coffee?

Cream or sugar?

Would you like to see a menu?

Would you care to see the wine list?

Are you ready to order?

Do you need a few more minutes (to decide what you want)?

Would you like to see the menu again for dessert?

419   Reciting special meal offers for the day

Let me tell you about our specials today.

The special of the day is roast beef and brown gravy with potatoes and two vegetables.

The specials are listed on the board.

The specials are on the right side (of the menu).

420   When a restaurant is out of some item

I'm sorry, we're out of that.

Sorry, it's all gone.

The chef informs me we're out of that. (*formal*)

421   Questions asked of a restaurant customer

How would you like that prepared?

How would you like your steak prepared?

How would you like your steak?

How would you like that done?

How would you like that?

What kind of potatoes would you like?

Mashed, boiled, hash browns, or french fries?

Would you like a baked potato, fries, or rice?

That comes with a salad.

Would you like soup or salad with that?

Soup or salad?

The soup of the day is split pea or chicken noodle.

Our dressings are Ranch, Italian, Thousand Island, Greek, and house.

> *house = the standard dressing used in this restaurant*

Would you like some fresh ground pepper?

Say when.

> *= Speak when you have had enough.*

422   Requesting something to drink at a restaurant

Coffee, please.

I'd like some coffee.

I'd like some decaf.

> *decaf = decaffeinated coffee*

I'd like an espresso.

I'd like tea.

Just coffee for the moment.

Just coffee for now.

Black coffee.

Coffee with cream.

Cream and sugar.

Can you get me a glass of water?

Could we have some water, please?

423   Requesting attention from a waiter or waitress

Can you come here when you have a second?

Oh, waiter!

Oh, miss!

Excuse me, ma'am.

Pardon me.

Excuse me.

424 Explaining to a waiter or waitress that you are not ready to order

We need a couple more minutes to decide.

I need a few more minutes to decide.

Could I see a menu, please?

I'm not ready to order yet.

I haven't figured out what I want yet.

I haven't decided yet.

425 Indicating readiness to order a meal at a restaurant

We're ready to order.

Can we order now?

Can you take our orders now?

We're ready.

426 Asking about specific items on a restaurant menu

What are the specials?

What is the special of the day?

Do you have any specials?

What would you suggest?

Do you have any recommendations?

What's good today?

What does that come with?

What comes with that?

Does that come with a salad?

What kind of dressing do you have?

Do you have any lo-cal dressing?

    lo-cal = low calorie

What's the soup of the day?

Is that prepared with meat?

Is there meat in that?

Do you have vegetarian dishes?

427 Requesting that certain foods not be served to you in a restaurant

No mayo(nnaise), please.

mayo(nnaise) ≈ nuts, onions, garlic, lettuce, bacon, pickles, etc.

No mayo.

Hold the mayo.

Leave off the mayo.

428 Concerning food allergies when ordering at a restaurant

I'd like that without MSG, please.

MSG = monosodium glutamate, typically used in Chinese food

Does this contain MSG?

Does this contain nuts?

I cannot tolerate nuts. I'm allergic.

No nuts. I'm allergic.

No MSG, please.

I'm allergic to dairy products.

I'm allergic to wheat.

429 Telling how a steak is to be cooked in a restaurant

I'd like my steak well-done.

well-done = completely cooked

I'd like my steak rare.

rare = partially cooked

I'd like my steak medium.

medium = between rare and well-done

Please make sure it's well-done.

I'd like my steak medium-well.

I want the steak thoroughly cooked.

I'd like my steak medium-rare.

Can I get it rare?

430   Requesting additional servings in a restaurant

I need more coffee.

Could I have more coffee, please?

Could I have some more bread, please?

Could I have some more water, please?

More bread, please. (*informal*)

Could I have some more butter?

431   Ordering wine in a restaurant

May I see the wine list?

Could I see your wine list?

I'd like a glass of wine.

I'd like a carafe of wine.

We'd like to order a bottle of wine.

432   Making a complaint in a restaurant

I can't eat this.

This meat is too fatty.

This meat is too tough.

This meat isn't fresh.

This fish isn't fresh.

I didn't order this.

These vegetables are hardly cooked at all.

The vegetables are overcooked and mushy.

This is cold. Can you take it back to the kitchen?

Could I speak with the manager, please?

433 **Asking about the location of a rest room in a public building**

Is there somewhere I could wash my hands?

Where are the public rest rooms?

Where is the washroom?

Where is the men's room?

Where is the ladies' room?

Where would I find the rest rooms?

Where's the john? (*informal*)

> *the john = the toilet; a rest room*

434 **Ordering food to be taken out**

Do you have carryout?

I would like to order something to carry out.

Can I get that to go?

To go, please.

435 **Requests to have uneaten food wrapped so it can be taken home**

Could you wrap this, please?

Could we have a doggie bag?

> *a doggie bag = a special bag or container for taking uneaten food home from a restaurant (as if it were being taken home to feed the dog)*

I'd like to take the rest.

I'd like to take the rest home.

436 **When your food is brought to the table in a restaurant**

Here's your order.

There you go.

Careful, the plate is hot.

Enjoy your meal.

Enjoy. (*informal*)

437 Asking for a diner's opinion of a meal

I hope that everything is satisfactory.

Is everything all right?

Is everything OK?

How are you doing?

Are you enjoying your meal?

How's your steak?

How's that steak?

438 A waiter or waitress seeking to be of further service

More coffee?

Is there anything I can get for you?

Is there anything I can get you?

Is there anything else?

Is there anything else I can get for you this evening?
  (*formal*)

Is there anything else I can get for you?

Anything else I can do for you?

439 A waiter or waitress offering dessert

Would you care for dessert?

Would you like to try one of our desserts?

Would you like to see the dessert menu?

Would you like to see the menu again?

Let me show you the dessert tray.

440 Asking for the bill in a restaurant

Could I have the bill?

Could I have the check?

We'd like the bill, please.

Check, please.

Separate checks, please.

Do I pay you or the cashier?

Do you take this (credit card)?

Can I have a receipt, please?

May I have a receipt, please? (*formal*)

We are ready to leave now.

All together.

All on one (check).

441 About payment for a meal in a restaurant

Is this all on one bill?

Separate checks?

You can pay at the register.

You can pay me.

I'll take it when you're ready.

442 Concerning the payment of a bill in a restaurant

There seems to be a mistake.

We did not order this item.

Does this include the tip?

Does this include a gratuity?

Is a gratuity included?

Keep the change.

BARS

443 A bartender asking what you want

What's yours?

What'll you have?

May I help you?

What'll it be, friend? (*informal*)

Another (of the same)?

444 Asking what's available at a bar

What (beer) do you have on tap?

> *on tap = ready to be drawn from a keg*

What kind of beer do you have?

What beers ya got? (*informal*)

What (beer) do you have on draft?

>   *on draft = ready to be drawn from a keg*

What kinds of wine do you have?

Do you have any imported beer?

445　Requesting a glass or bottle of beer

I'll have a beer.

>   *I'll have ≈ Please give me, Give me, I'll take, Make mine, Gimme, Do you have (?)*

I'll have a Bud.

>   *Bud ≈ Miller's, Budweiser, Heinekens, Mich(alob), Special Export, Coor's, etc.*

I'll have a draft.

>   *a draft = a beer drawn from a keg, or a bottle of beer with Draft in the brand name*

Make it a cold one.

>   *a cold one = a cold beer*

Pour me a beer. (*informal*)

Give me a beer. (*informal*)

446　Various requests for drinks from a bartender

I'd like (some) coffee.

>   *I'd like ≈ Can I please have (?), I'll take, Please get me*

I'd like (some) coffee with cream.

I'd like (some) coffee with sugar.

I'd like (some) coffee with cream and sugar.

I'd like a Coke.

I'd like some Coke.

I'd like a diet cola.

I'd like a mineral water.

I'd like a beer.

I'd like a glass of beer.

I'd like a stein of beer.

I'd like a pitcher of beer.

I'd like a light beer.

I'd like a dark beer.

I'd like a domestic beer.

I'd like a draft beer.

I'd like an ale.

I'd like a lager.

I'd like a glass of wine.

I'd like some champagne.

I'd like a scotch.

I'd like a scotch on the rocks.

I'd like a whiskey with soda.

I'd like a gin and tonic.

I'd like a gin and tonic with a twist.

447   Special instructions to a bartender

Make it dry.

> = *I prefer a dry Martini or a dry wine.*

Hold the cherry.

Give me another.

I'll have another (one) of the same.

> *the same = the same as previously ordered*

I'll have the same.

Two olives, please.

I'd like it on the rocks.

> *on the rocks = with ice cubes*

Make that on the rocks.

448   Buying drinks with friends

I'm buying.

Let me get this (one).

It's on me.

on me = on my account = I'm paying

The next round is on me.

round = an order of drinks for everyone

No, no, this one's on me!

This is my round.

This round's on me.

It's on me.

I'm buying.

Who's buying?

Want to run a tab?

a tab = a running account

449   Charges for drinks at a bar

That'll be six bucks.

Do you wish to pay me now?

Would you like to start a tab?

You've run up quite a tab.

You really have to pay something on your bill.

450   Expressions used with friends at a bar asking about drinks

What are we having?

Do you all want to get a pitcher?

Anyone for a pizza?

Name your poison.

What'll you have?

What's yours?

Care for another?

451   Expressions about drinking additional drinks

I'm going to drown my sorrows.

Let's have another round.

Let's have a nightcap.

> *a nightcap = a final drink of the evening*

Let's knock back another.

Let's toss one back.

452   Asking for a small drink of beverage alcohol

I'll have just a nip.

> *a nip = a swallow*

I'll have just a sip.

I'll have a shot.

> *a shot = a swallow; a jigger*

Give me a swig.

> *a swig = a swallow*

Give me a hit.

> *a hit = a swallow*

Give me a jigger.

> *a jigger = 1.5 ounces; a 1.5-ounce glass*

453   Encouraging someone to drink

That'll put hair on your chest. (*idiomatic*)

> *= The drink is strong and it will invigorate you.*

Let's tie one on. (*slang*)

> *= Let's get drunk.*

That'll knock your socks off. (*idiomatic*)

> *= The drink is very strong and it will shock your system.*

This'll wet your whistle. (*idiomatic*)

> *= This drink will quench your thirst.*

Let's get down to some serious drinking. (*informal*)

> *= Let's get drunk together.*

Have a hair of the dog that bit you. (*cliché*)

> *= Have some more of what made you drunk.*

Let's paint the town red. (*cliché*)

> *= Let's celebrate.*

Party down! (*slang*)

Party hearty! (*slang*)

Party hardy! (*slang*)

454   Asking about the time that a bar closes

Is it closing time already?

Last call already?

> *last call = the announcement of the last opportunity to purchase a drink before closing time*

When do we have to be out of here?

When's last call?

455   Encouraging someone to finish a drink

Drain it.

Drink up.

Have one for the road.

Pound it and let's go. (*slang*)

456   Drinking toasts

Here's looking at you.

Here's mud in your eye.

Here's to you.

Here's to us.

To your health!

To John V. Jones!

Cheers!

Down the hatch!

Bottoms up!

Drink up!

To life!

457   When someone drinks too much

I think that this is your last one.

I think you've had enough.

That's all for you, Bud. (*informal*)

Haven't you had about enough?

Do you really think you ought to have another one?

458   Stating that someone is drunk

He's feeling no pain. (*informal*)

He's drunk as a skunk. (*informal*)

He's three sheets to the wind. (*informal*)

He's stone drunk.

He's tanked. (*slang*)

He's pickled. (*slang*)

He's as drunk as a lord. (*informal*)

BAKERY

459   Placing an order for baked goods

I'd like a dozen donuts, please.

> *I'd like* ≈ *Could I please have (?), I need, Please give me, Let me have*

I'd like a glazed donut.

I'd like a cream-filled pastry, please.

I'd like a raspberry danish.

I'd like a long john.

I'd like a sugar twist.

I'd like a chocolate donut and a cup of coffee.

I'd like a big box of donut holes.

> *a donut hole = a piece of donut pastry made from the part that was removed to make the hole in a donut*

I'd like to order a cake.

I'd like a dozen cookies.

I'd like a loaf of rye bread.

I'd like two dozen onion bagels, please.

> *bagels = circular bread rolls*

I'd like a dozen assorted donuts, please.

460   Placing an order at a bakery for something to drink

I'd like a cup of coffee to go.

> *I'd like ≈ Could I please have (?), I need, Please give me, Let me have*

I'd like a decaffeinated coffee.

> *decaffeinated = without caffeine*

I'd like some decaffeinated coffee.

I'd like a decaf.

> *a decaf = a cup of decaffeinated coffee*

Could I have a soda?

I'd like some decaf.

I'd like some milk.

461   Taking out a bakery order or eating it in the shop

I will eat it here.

It's for here.

To go. (*informal*)

I'd like that to go.

462   Special orders in a bakery

Sliced (bread), please.

Do you do special icings?

What kind of bread do you have?

What kind of bagels do you have?

Do you bake birthday cakes to order?

HOME COOKING

463   Stating that you are hungry

I'm hungry.

I'm famished.

I'm starved.

I'm ravenous.

My mouth is watering.

That stew is mouth-watering.

I'm so hungry I could eat a horse.

I could eat a horse. (*cliché*)

I'm (just) dying of hunger.

464   Asking when a meal will be ready

When do we eat?

When's chow? (*slang*)

When's dinner?

When's supper?

When will supper be ready?

465   Asking what is for dinner

What's to eat?

What's for supper?

What are we having?

466   Stating when food will be ready

Dinner's almost ready.

It's almost done.

It will be on the table in a minute.

It's almost ready.

(It's) time to eat.

It's time to sit down.

Dinner's ready.

Please be seated at the table.

Dinner is served. (*formal*)

Soup's on! (*informal*)

  = *Dinner's ready!*

467   Offering someone a bit of food

Would you like a taste?

How about a bite?

Would you like a bite?

Want a taste?

468   Blessing the food

Who wants to say grace?

Shall we say grace? (*formal*)

Shall we pray? (*formal*)

Let's pray.

Let us pray. (*formal*)

469   Concerning passing food at the table

Please pass me the salt.

Please pass the pepper.

Please pass the butter.

Could you pass the rolls around?

Could you start the rolls around?

Could you start the rolls going around?

Could I have some gravy?

Would you like the salt and pepper?

Would you care for the butter?

Would you care for some butter?

Pardon my boardinghouse reach. (*informal*)

> boardinghouse reach = a long and somewhat impolite
> reach for something at the table

470   Concerning additional servings of food

Could you pour me some more milk?

More milk, please.

Could I have seconds, please?

May I have seconds, please?

Would you like some more of this?

Is there any more of this?

What's for dessert?

471 Enforcing good table manners

Don't put your elbows on the table.

Don't talk with your mouth full.

Don't read at the table.

No TV during dinner.

> *TV = television*

Wipe your mouth.

Put your napkin on your lap.

Put your napkin in your lap.

472 Cleaning up after a meal

Can you help me with the dishes?

Please carry your own dishes to the kitchen.

I'll wash and you dry.

I'll scrape and you load (the dishwasher).

473 Excusing oneself from the table

Do you mind if I leave the table?

> *(said by an adult)*

I'll have to excuse myself.

> *(said by an adult)*

May I please leave the table?

> *(said by a child)*

May I be excused?

> *(said by a child)*

474 Encouraging children to eat

Finish your food.

Be quiet and eat your dinner.

Be quiet and eat your food.

You have to clean up your plate.

If you don't eat your vegetables, you won't get any dessert.

There are starving children in Africa. (*cliché*)

> *Africa ≈ Bosnia, Asia, South America, etc.*

HEALTH

HEALTH AND APPEARANCE

475   When someone is in good health

His doctor gave him a clean bill of health.

> *a clean bill of health = a good report on one's health*

He's the picture of health.

He's in the pink.

He looks great.

He's looking good.

He's in top form.

He's at the top of his form.

I couldn't be better.

I feel like a million dollars.

I feel like a million bucks.

She looks like a million dollars.

She looks like a million bucks.

He's bright-eyed and bushy-tailed. (*idiomatic*)

I'm sound as a dollar. (*cliché*)

I'm fresh as a daisy. (*cliché*)

She's healthy as a horse. (*cliché*)

She's fit as a fiddle. (*cliché*)

476   Observing that someone looks disorderly

You look tired.

You look like you need some sleep.

You look dreadful.

You look terrible.

You look like hell. (*mildly vulgar*)

You look a sight.
You're a sight.
Look what the cat dragged in. (*informal*)
You look like something the cat dragged in. (*informal*)
You look like you've been to hell and back. (*informal*)
You look like you've been through a war.
You look like you've gone through the wringer.

477 When someone looks very bad
You could stop a truck. (*informal*)
You could stop a clock. (*informal*)
That face could stop a clock. (*informal*)
Are you having a bad hair day? (*informal*)
You're as ugly as sin. (*informal*)

478 Inquiring about someone's health or well-being
Are you OK?
Are you feeling OK?
Are you all right?
Do you feel all right?

479 When someone does not look well
You don't look well.
You don't look too good. (*informal*)
You don't look so good. (*informal*)
You look like death.
You look like death warmed over.
You look green around the gills.
You look a little peaked.
You look flushed.
You look pale.
You're pale.
You're white as a ghost.

SICKNESS

480   **Concerning allergies**

I'm allergic to sulfa.

I'm allergic to ≈ I have an allergy to, I can't tolerate

I'm allergic to penicillin.

I'm allergic to cats.

I'm allergic to dogs.

I'm allergic to pollen.

I'm allergic to dust.

I'm allergic to bees.

I'm allergic to bee stings.

I'm allergic to chocolate.

I'm allergic to shrimp.

I'm allergic to strawberries.

I can't have chocolate.

I can't eat strawberries.

I can't drink milk.

I can't have dairy products.

I can't digest milk.

I'm lactose intolerant.

I have hayfever.

Dairy products make me break out in a rash.

My ID bracelet lists my allergies.

ID = identification

I have an environmental illness.

481   **Allergic problems with the nose and breathing**

My allergies are acting up.

My sinuses are acting up.

My sinuses are bothering me.

My sinuses are congested.

My sinuses ache.

My nose is clogged.

My nose is stuffed up.

My nose is congested.

I can't breathe.

482 When someone sneezes

Bless you.

God bless you.

Gesundheit. (*German*)

483 Allergic problems with the eyes

My eyes are swollen.

My eyes are puffy.

My eyes itch.

My eyes are itchy.

484 Allergic problems with the skin

My skin is breaking out.

I'm breaking out.

I'm breaking out in hives.

I break out when I eat chocolate.

My skin itches whenever I eat shrimp.

485 Expressing general feelings of illness

I'm sick.

I feel sick.

I'm sick as a dog. (*informal*)

I feel funny.

I feel awful.

I feel downright awful.

I feel terrible.

I feel lousy.

I feel rotten.

I feel like hell. (*mildly vulgar*)

486   Expressing mild discomfort owing to illness

I don't feel well.

I don't feel so well.

I don't feel quite right.

I feel ill.

I'm not feeling myself.

I'm feeling under the weather.

I'm a little under the weather.

I'm feeling a little down in the mouth.

487   When you feel like vomiting

I feel sick to my stomach.

I'm sick to my stomach.

I feel nauseous.

I feel like throwing up. (*informal*)

I think I'm going to throw up. (*informal*)

I think I'm going to vomit.

I'm going to barf. (*slang*)

    to barf = to vomit

I think I'm going to be sick.

    to be sick = to vomit

I think I'm going to lose my cookies. (*slang*)

    to lose my cookies = to vomit

I think I'm going to lose my lunch. (*slang*)

    to lose my lunch = to vomit

488   Describing a pain in the head

I have a headache.

My head hurts.

My head is killing me.

I've got a splitting headache.

My head is throbbing.

My head is pounding.

There's a hammering inside my head.

I have a migraine.

I have an excruciating headache.

489   Describing dizziness

I'm dizzy.

The room is spinning.

I'm so dizzy I can't stand up.

I'm so dizzy I have to sit down.

490   Describing being exhausted or worn-out

I'm exhausted.

I need some rest.

I need a nap.

I need to take a day off.

I need a day off.

I need a vacation.

My get-up-and-go has got up and left. (*informal*)

 get-up-and-go = energy; vitality

491   Offering care to a sick person

Can I get you a glass of water?

Do you want a glass of water?

Would you like a glass of water?

Would a glass of water help?

Would you like to lie down?

Want to lie down?

Would you like some aspirin?

Want some aspirin?

Should I call a doctor?

Have you seen a doctor?

492   Concerning catching a disease

Is it catching?

Are you contagious?

Don't give it to me.

I don't want to catch it.

You need to relax.

You've been running around too much.

Your resistance is down.

It's been going around.

DOCTORS

493 Questions a doctor asks of a patient

What's the matter?

What brings you here?

Describe what's wrong.

What seems to be the problem?

You look fit as a fiddle. What could be wrong?

Can you describe the problem?

Can you describe the symptoms?

Can you tell me what's wrong?

Does it hurt when I do this?

Has this been a problem before?

Have you had this problem before?

Have you had this problem long?

How long have you had this problem?

Have you had this before?

494 Getting your medical history

Is your mother living?

Is your father living?

What did your mother die of?

What did your father die of?

Is there a history of diabetes in your family?

> *diabetes ≈ cancer, heart disease, arthritis, strokes*

495   Telling the doctor what happened

I fell down the stairs.

I fell off a skateboard.

I got hit with a ball.

I got hit with a bat.

I was in a fight.

I was in an accident.

496   Telling the doctor about a pain in the back

I have a pain in my back.

My back is sore.

I can't bend over.

I can't get up.

My back hurts.

I have an aching back.

I pulled my back.

I threw my back out.

497   Telling the doctor about soreness

I pulled a muscle.

I strained a muscle.

I sprained my wrist.

I twisted my ankle.

My ankle is swollen.

It's all red and puffy.

498   Telling the doctor about bleeding

I'm bleeding.

It keeps bleeding.

It won't stop bleeding.

I'm bleeding like a stuck pig. (*informal*)

499 **Telling the doctor about various pains and problems**

There's a kink in my neck.

a kink = a twist or cramp

There's a crick in my back.

a crick = a muscle spasm

I have a lump here.

It stings.

I've got a stinging sensation.

I feel weak.

I feel dizzy.

I feel feverish.

I'm having hot flashes.

I get the chills.

I can't put pressure on my foot.

I can't step down on my foot.

It burns when I go to the bathroom.

My eyes hurt in bright light.

My ears hurt when it's noisy.

My arm hurts when I move it like this.

It hurts here.

It hurts when I run.

It hurts after I eat.

It hurts when I breathe.

It hurts when I do this.

500 **Telling the doctor how long you have been ill**

I've been sick for a day.

I've been sick for two weeks.

I lost my appetite four days ago.

This started a week ago.

501 Telling the doctor about vomiting

I've been throwing up.

I can't hold food down.

I lose my cookies. (*slang*)

I lose my lunch. (*slang*)

I've got morning sickness.

   morning sickness = nausea associated with pregnancy

502 Telling the doctor about bowel problems

I've got diarrhea.

I've got the runs.

I'm constipated.

503 Telling the doctor about sleep problems

I can't sleep.

I have insomnia.

I lie awake all night long.

I've been really sleepy.

I'm always drowsy.

I can't seem to stay awake.

504 Telling the doctor about allergies

My skin itches.

I have a rash.

I've got blotches all over my skin.

I've got these bumps on my skin.

I'm allergic to penicillin.

I'm allergic to sulfa.

I'm diabetic.

I'm asthmatic.

I have asthma.

505 Important things to tell a doctor

I'm pregnant.

I think I'm pregnant.

I'm on medication.

I have a heart condition.

I have a pacemaker.

I have arthritis.

I am allergic to penicillin.

I've had this before.

This problem runs in the family.

All my father's relatives have this disease.

506 Expressions a doctor uses about medicine and tests

Do you have any allergies?

Are you allergic to any medications?

Are you allergic to penicillin?

I'm going to write you a prescription.

I'm going to give you a prescription.

I'm going to give you something for it.

I'm going to give you something for the pain.

I'd like to run some tests.

When was the last time you had a tetanus shot?

I'd like to take a blood sample.

I should have the results back in a week.

The results should be back in a week.

I'm going to refer you to someone else.

Take two aspirin and call me in the morning.

507 Asking a doctor about a medical problem

Can it be cured?

Is it serious?

Is it broken?

Is it malignant?

Is it cancer?

Is it curable?

Is it treatable?

Can you do something about it?
Do I need stitches?
Do I need surgery?
Will my insurance cover this?
Do I have to stay overnight?

508   **Talking to a hospital patient**
Are you all right?
How are you feeling today?
Are you doing better today?
You look good.
You're looking really good.
You're looking well.
Your color is good.
I brought you some flowers.
I brought you some candy.
I came as soon as I heard.
I got here as soon as I could.
John sends his love.
Get well soon.

509   **Questions for the hospital patient**
Have they figured out what's wrong?
What's the prognosis?

> *the prognosis = the prediction for the future outcome
> of an illness*

How long will you be here?
When do you get to go home?
When are you going home?
When are you being released?
Is there anything you need?
Do you need anything?
Is there anything I can do?

Can I get you anything?
Should I call for the nurse?
Is the food as bad as they say?
How's the food?
How's your doctor?

510 Explaining that your health is improving
I'm improving.
I'm getting better.
I'm getting over it.
I'm getting back on my feet.
I'm getting back on my legs.
I'm getting back to normal.
I'm bouncing back.
I'm on the road to recovery.
I'm out of the woods.
Things are looking up.
I've hit bottom and things are looking up.
I'm better now.
I'm better than I was.

511 Explaining that you are receiving medical care
I still have to go back to the doctor for a follow-up.
I'm still under a doctor's care.
I'm still seeing a doctor.
I'm in therapy.
I'm still seeing a therapist.

512 Explaining that you are cured of a health problem
I'm well now.
I'm all better.
I'm completely over it.
I'm as good as new.

It's like it never happened.

I feel like a new person.

I've got a new lease on life.

MEDICINE

513 Instructions for taking prescription medication

One teaspoon daily.

One teaspoon three times daily.

One tablet three times daily.

Two capsules three times daily.

Take three times daily.

Take four times daily.

Take in the morning.

Take before going to bed.

Take as needed.

Take two of the pills each morning for two weeks.

Not to be taken more than four times within a 24-hour period.

Take after eating.

Take before eating.

This medication should be taken with meals.

This medication should be taken with food.

Do not eat for half an hour before or after taking this medicine.

Do not operate heavy machinery while taking this medication.

Do not drink alcohol.

Do not drive after taking this medication.

514 Medical warnings and advice found on product labels

Pregnant women: please consult your physician before use.

Attention phenylketonurics: contains phenylalanine.

Warning: The U.S. Surgeon General has determined that smoking is hazardous to your health.

Sodium content provided for customers who, on the advice of a physician, are modifying their sodium intake.

May cause drowsiness.

Contains MSG.

Expires 10/15/98.

Use before 10/15/98.

515 Health claims found on consumer products
Low fat.
Fat-free.
Contains no cholesterol.
Contains low sodium.
Low sodium.

MENTAL HEALTH

516 Statements made to a guidance counselor or therapist
I need help.
I've been depressed lately.
I've been thinking about killing myself.
I've been thinking about suicide.
I've been suicidal.
I've been considering suicide.
I'm lonely.
I'm scared.
I'm stressed out at work. (*informal*)
I'm under a lot of stress.
I'm under a lot of pressure.
I get really nervous in public.
I'm very anxious.
I'm really anxious.

I hear voices.

I see things that really aren't there.

No one likes me.

No one loves me.

My boss hates me.

I hate my parents.

I hate my kids.

I hate my job.

I hate my boss.

I dread going to work.

I dread going home.

I'm hostile toward my parents.

I don't know what's wrong with me.

I can't describe it, really.

I can't express my anger.

I'm afraid to let my emotions show.

I'm afraid that people will laugh at me.

I let people walk all over me.

I get taken advantage of.

I let people take advantage of me.

I let myself be taken advantage of.

I can't say no.

I'm not assertive enough.

I'm not aggressive enough.

517   Statements concerning excessive drinking

I drink to excess.

I drink excessively.

I get drunk almost every day.

I probably drink more than I should.

I guess I drink more than most people I know.

I drink too much.

I've been drinking too much.

I am an alcoholic.

518 **Statements about sexual and physical abuse**

I was molested as a child.

I was abused as a child.

I was sexually abused as a child.

My husband beats me.

I beat my children.

519 **Statements made to a marriage counselor**

The romance has gone out of our marriage.

The honeymoon is over.

I've fallen out of love.

I don't love her anymore.

She doesn't love me anymore.

We've drifted apart.

It's the little things that annoy me.

He never listens to me.

We never talk anymore.

He doesn't pay any attention to me.

He's always yelling.

He's never there when I need him.

He's always out with his friends.

520 **Statements made about infidelity**

I found out she was having an affair.

I found out he was seeing someone behind my back.

I found out he was seeing someone else.

She's seeing someone on the side.

   on the side = in addition

She's got someone on the side.

He's found somebody else.

She's found somebody new.

He's been fooling around. (*informal*)

    fooling around = being unfaithful

She's been messing around. (*informal*)

    messing around = being unfaithful

521   **Statements made about trying to make a marriage work**

We'd like to try to make it work.

We'd like to work it out.

We'd like to stay together.

GETTING A JOB

522   **Questions found on surveys and forms**
Name?
Address?
Phone?
Occupation?
Previous occupation?
Income level?
Education level?
Sex?
Gender?
  = Sex?
Race?
Ethnic group?
Religion?
Church affiliation?
Age?
DOB?
  = Date of birth?
Date of birth?
SSN?
  = Social Security Number?
Social Security Number?
Marital status?
Account number?
Comments?

523 **A prospective employee to a prospective employer during an interview**

What's the salary?

Is it salaried or hourly?

Is it part-time or full-time?

What are the hours?

What are the benefits?

Do I get insurance?

What would be expected of me?

What are you looking for (in an employee)?

524 **An employer to a prospective employee during an interview**

What are your qualifications?

What is your degree in?

Where did you go to school?

What sort of salary do you expect?

Let me see your résumé.

Let me see your dossier.

> *a dossier = a résumé = a list of one's accomplishments*

Let me see your references.

Do you have a portfolio?

> *a portfolio = a collection of samples of one's work*

Why did you leave your last job?

When can you start?

We will call you if we need you.

Don't call us; we'll call you. (*cliché*)

525 **A prospective employee to a human resources or personnel director**

I want to fill out an insurance form.

> *I want ≈ I need, I would like*

I want to change my insurance coverage.

I want to change my withholding (tax).

I want to schedule my vacation days for this year.

526   An employee to a human resources or personnel director

I'd like to set up a training session for my department.

  I'd like ≈ I need, I want, I have, I would like

I'd like to book the audio/visual room for today.

I'd like to schedule a meeting in the conference room.

I'd like some information on the alcohol awareness program.

I'd like some information on the substance abuse program.

I'd like to take a leave of absence.

I'd like to be considered for the opening in the accounting department.

  accounting ≈ credit, editorial, auditing, sales, etc.

Here's my expense report.

I think there was a mistake in my last paycheck.

527   Complaining to a human resources or personnel director

I'd like to file a complaint.

I'm not getting along with one of my co-workers.

My boss has been harassing me.

My boss has been sexually harassing me.

I'm being discriminated against.

528   Describing a lack of work experience

You haven't had much experience (in this line of work).

You are still a little new to all this.

You're a little green. (*idiomatic*)

  green = new; fresh to the job

You're still wet behind the ears. (*idiomatic*)

  wet behind the ears = new to this

You're still young.
You're still new.
You'll catch on.
Give it time.

529 Concerning an easy task or employment position

I can do that.

No sweat. (*slang*)

> = *Not difficult.*

Simple.

Simplicity itself.

Nothing to it.

(It's) a piece of cake. (*slang*)

> *a piece of cake = easy*

I could do that with my eyes closed.

I could do that with one arm tied behind my back.

I could do that standing on my head.

I could do that in my sleep.

It's easy as pie. (*cliché*)

> *pie = eating pie*

It's easy as ABC.

It's as easy as falling off a log. (*cliché*)

It's water off a duck's back. (*cliché*)

It's like taking candy from a baby.

It's second nature.

It's like breathing.

530 Making claims about your competence and ability

I wrote the book on that. (*idiomatic*)

> = *I am an authority on that.*

I know it like a book. (*idiomatic*)

I know it like the back of my hand. (*cliché*)

I know whereof I speak.

> = *I know what I'm talking about.*

I know all the tricks of the trade. (*idiomatic*)

> *the tricks of the trade = the ways to do things correctly*

I know it backwards and forwards.

I know it inside and out.

I know my math.

> *math ≈ carpentry, cooking, history, computers, etc.*

It's my job.

I'm a professional.

I'm an old hand at this. (*idiomatic*)

> *an old hand = an experienced worker*

I've been there.

I've paid my dues.

The stories I could tell you!

You want to hear about my battle scars?

> *= Want to hear about my past experiences and problems?*

531   Describing your thoroughness

I've run the gamut.

I've run the gamut from A to Z.

I know it all from A to Z.

I've traveled the globe from pole to pole.

I've traveled the states from sea to shining sea.

I've traveled the country from sea to shining sea.

I've looked high and low for you.

> *high and low = everywhere*

I've been to hell and back again. (*cliché, mildly vulgar*)

> *to hell and back = everywhere*

I've been to hell and back. (*mildly vulgar*)

I've been to the end of the earth and back. (*cliché*)

I searched this room from top to bottom.

> *from top to bottom = thoroughly*

I slept from dusk to dawn.

I worked from dawn to dusk.

I worked from sunup to sundown.

HOLDING A JOB

532   Reprimanding an employee

You're late.

You're late again.

Try to be on time next time.

Let's try to be here on time.

Let's try to get here on time.

Don't be late.

533   Inviting an employee into a private office for a reprimand

May I have a word with you? (*formal*)

Might I have a word with you? (*formal*)

Could I have a word with you?

Could I see you in my office?

I'll see you in my office in ten minutes.

534   Praising an employee

Good work.

Keep up the good work.

Nice work.

Nice job.

Very nice.

Very impressive.

I've been hearing some good things about you.

You keep this up and you are going to get a raise.

We are very pleased with your work.

535   Explaining why you are having difficulty in a new job

I'm sorry, I've never done this before.

This is all so new to me.

I'm new at this.

I'm a newcomer to this.

This is a first for me.

I'll get onto this yet. (*informal*)

Oh, well. You can't lose them all. (*informal*)

536 Excuses for failure or offense

I'm just following orders.

I was only following orders.

That's the way I was told to do it.

That's the way we've always done it.

I'm doing the best I can.

I'm doing my best.

I'm doing my very best.

You can't get blood from a turnip. (*cliché*)

There are only so many hours in a day.

> = *There is a limited amount of time in the day for work.*

537 Explaining why you are not going to do something

It's not in my job description.

It's not my job.

It's not my responsibility.

I have no training in that area.

I am not competent to do that.

538 Approaching a deadline

I have a deadline to meet.

This deadline is looming large on the horizon. (*cliché*)

I've got to crank out this project tonight. (*informal*)

I'm under the gun. (*informal*)

> *under the gun* = *under pressure*

It's getting down to the wire. (*idiomatic*)

> *down to the wire = close to the finish, as in a horse race*

It's down to the wire. (*idiomatic*)

I'm running out of time.

I'm going to need an extension (of the deadline).

539   Conveying urgency

I need it now.

I need it immediately.

I need it in a flash. (*informal*)

> *in a flash = in a big hurry*

I need it in a jiffy. (*informal*)

> *in a jiffy = in a big hurry*

I need it in two shakes (of a lamb's tail). (*informal*)

> *in two shakes of a lamb's tail = very fast*

I need it yesterday.

540   Telling someone to hurry

Hurry up!

Hurry!

Get moving!

Get going!

Get cracking! (*slang*)

Get the lead out! (*slang*)

Get your ass in gear! (*mildly vulgar*)

Get a move on. (*informal*)

Get on it. (*informal*)

Get right on this.

Get with it. (*informal*)

Get on with it. (*informal*)

Shake a leg! (*informal*)

> = *Get your legs moving!*

Snap to it! (*informal*)

Make it snappy! (*informal*)

    snappy = fast

Look alive! (*informal*)

Step on it! (*informal*)

Make it quick! (*informal*)

Double time!

    = Twice as fast!

On the double! (*informal*)

Chop, chop! (*informal*)

Go! (*informal*)

Drop everything (and do it)!

This is top priority.

This is priority one.

This is a rush job.

(There's) no time like the present. (*cliché*)

Let's get the show on the road. (*idiomatic*)

Let's get this show on the road. (*idiomatic*)

541   **Encouraging someone to keep working at a job**

You'll get the hang of it eventually.

    to get the hang of it = to learn how to do it; to get used to it

You'll get the knack of it.

    the knack of it = the way to do it

You'll pick it up as you go along.

    to pick it up = to learn it

You'll learn more as you go along.

BUSINESS MEETINGS

542   **Expressions used under parliamentary procedure**

I'd like to call the meeting to order.

This meeting is called to order.

Will the clerk please read the minutes of the last meeting?

the minutes = the official record of a previous meeting

I move that the minutes be approved.

The chair recognizes Mr. Smith.

the chair = the presiding officer of a meeting

Mrs. Jones has the floor.

*has the floor = is officially and exclusively permitted
to address the group for a piece of business*

You have not been recognized.

recognized = called on; given the floor

Please address the chair.

= Please direct your remarks to the presiding officer.

Please address the chairman.

*the chairman ≈ the chairperson, the chair, the
chairwoman*

Point of order.

You're out of order.

Will the secretary please strike that last remark from the
record?

543 Concerning motions under parliamentary procedure

I'd like to make a motion.

a motion = a formal proposal to be voted on

I'd like to move that we accept the proposal.

I move that we accept the proposal.

A motion has been made. Is there a second?

a second = an endorsement from an additional person

I second that motion.

All those in favor, say aye.

aye = yes

All those opposed, say nay.

nay = no

All those opposed, say no.

Abstention.

> = *I choose not to vote*

Roll call vote, please.

Please confine your remarks to the motion before us.

I move to table the motion.

> *to table the motion = to delay consideration of the proposal*

I move to table the discussion.

I move we move this issue to committee.

I call the motion to question.

> = *I call for a vote on the motion.*

Question.

> = *Let's vote on the motion.*

544 Adjourning a meeting under parliamentary procedure

I move to adjourn the meeting.

The meeting is adjourned.

545 Expressions heard in negotiating sessions

Hear me out.

I'm willing to hear you out.

I'm more than willing to meet you halfway.

Try to avoid a no-win situation.

> *a no-win situation = a situation where no one wins*

Let's try for a win-win situation.

> *a win-win situation = a situation where there are no losers*

We're ready to deal.

We're willing to strike a bargain.

We're willing to compromise.

We'd like to offer a compromise.

We have a proposal.

Let's talk turkey. (*idiomatic*)

> *to talk turkey = to get serious*

Let's cut to the chase. (*idiomatic*)

> *= Let's get to the serious matters.*

What's the bottom line?

> *the bottom line = the end result; the final cost or profit*

That item is not negotiable.

We reject your latest offer.

That is unacceptable.

We've hit a stumbling block.

We've reached an impasse.

Negotiations have broken down.

PROJECTS

546   Beginning a new project or activity

Where do we begin?

How should we go about doing this?

What's the first step?

What's first on the agenda?

Let's organize a task force.

Who will be in charge?

We're on our way.

We're off and running.

We're off to a good start.

We've hit the ground running.

We're headed in the right direction.

We're off on the right foot.

We've laid a good foundation.

We've only just begun.

We're just getting our feet wet. (*idiomatic*)

> *getting our feet wet = just getting started*

We've made a good dent in it. (*idiomatic*)

It's a start.

You've got to begin somewhere.

I'd like to lay down a few ground rules.

547 Concerning the deceptively difficult

It's not as easy as it seems.

It's not as easy as it looks.

It's harder than it looks.

It's harder than you think.

Easier said than done.

There's more to it than meets the eye.

It's surprisingly difficult.

It's like looking for a needle in a haystack.

It's a real challenge.

548 Concerning the impossible

That won't work.

That'll never hold water.

= *That will never be operable.*

Never happen. (*informal*)

There's no way. (*informal*)

No can do. (*informal*)

549 Concerning futility

You're wasting your time.

You're wasting your energy.

You're wasting your effort.

It doesn't stand a chance.

It doesn't stand a chance in hell. (*mildly vulgar*)

There's not a chance in hell. (*mildly vulgar*)

It doesn't stand a snowball's chance in hell. (*mildly vulgar*)

When hell freezes over. (*mildly vulgar*)

= *Never.*

You're spinning your wheels. (*informal*)

You're (just) running around in circles.

You're beating a dead horse. (*informal*)

> beating a dead horse = *trying to activate or motivate something that is finished*

It isn't worth beating your brains out (for). (*informal*)

It's like looking for a needle in a haystack. (*cliché*)

It's fit for the junkyard.

It's headed for the junk heap. (*informal*)

550   When something is unimportant

It doesn't matter.

It makes no difference.

It makes no nevermind. (*folksy*)

> = *It doesn't matter to me.*

It don't make (me) no nevermind. (*folksy*)

It's six of one, half a dozen of the other.

> = *It doesn't matter which one or which way.*

It's not important.

It's not worthwhile.

It's not worth your while.

It's not worth a hill of beans. (*idiomatic*)

It's not worth mentioning.

It's not worth the trouble.

It's not worth it.

551   Ending a project

Get rid of it.

Finish it off.

Nip it in the bud.

Do it in. (*informal*)

86 it. (*slang*)

> 86 = nix = *to negate; to destroy*

Kill it. (*informal*)

Kill it off. (*informal*)

Wipe it out. (*informal*)

Wipe it off the map. (*informal*)

Sound the death knell. (*informal*)

> *the death knell = the sound of bells that signals an impending or recent death*

Put it out of its misery. (*informal*)

Pull the plug on it. (*slang*)

Pull the rug out from under it. (*informal*)

Put the skids on it. (*informal*)

Nuke it. (*slang*)

> = *Destroy it with a nuclear bomb.*

Throw it away.

Throw it out.

Pitch it. (*informal*)

Toss it. (*informal*)

Junk it. (*informal*)

Trash it. (*informal*)

Dump it. (*informal*)

Put it in the circular file. (*informal*)

> *the circular file = a (round) wastebasket*

File it in the circular bin. (*informal*)

> *the circular bin = the circular file; a (round) wastebasket*

File it. (*informal*)

552   Starting over again on a project

Back to the drawing board.

It's back to the drawing board.

Well, it's back to square one.

Well, it's back to basics.

Time to start over from scratch.

SHOPPING

STORES AND SHOPS

553   Asking about store hours

When are you open?

When do you open?

How late are you open (today)?

What are your hours?

Are you open on weekends?

Are you open on Saturday?

Are you open after five?

554   A salesperson greeting a customer

May I help you?

Can I help you?

Can I help you find something?

Can I help you with something?

Can I show you something?

Are you being helped?

Is someone waiting on you?

Is there anything I can help you with?

Is there anything I can help you with today?

Is there anything I can help you find today?

555   A salesperson offering help to a customer

If you need me, I'll be right here.

If you need any help, I'll be right here.

If you need me, my name's Linda.

If you need any help, my name's Linda.

If I can help you find anything, I'll be right over here.

If I can help you, just let me know.

There's a mirror over there.

The changing rooms are over there.

Only six items in the dressing room at a time.

Only six items allowed in the dressing rooms.

556   Questions a salesperson might ask a customer

What are you interested in?

Are you looking for something in particular?

Are you looking for anything in particular?

Do you have anything in mind?

Do you have something specific in mind?

Do you know what you want?

What size do you need?

Do you know what size you are?

557   Offering merchandise to a customer

I've got just your size.

I've got just what you're looking for.

I've got exactly what you need.

I have just the thing.

> *just the thing = exactly the right thing*

Have I got something for you! (*informal*)

May I suggest this?

That's on sale this week.

558   Offering additional help to a customer

Do you need anything to go with that?

Is there anything else I can interest you in?

Is there anything else I can get for you?

Is there anything else I can help you with?

What else can I do for you?

559   Finding things in a department store

Where is the men's shop?

Where is ladies' wear?

ladies' wear = women's clothing department

Where is the shoe department?

What floor is furniture on?

Where are the children's clothes?

Where's children's clothes? (*informal*)

Where can I find children's clothes?

Do you sell appliances here?

Where is the credit department?

Is there a public rest room here?

560   Shopping for something at a department store

I'm looking for something for my wife.

I'm looking for something for my husband.

It's a gift.

I need a size 34.

I don't know my size.

Can you measure me?

Would you measure my waist, please?

I need a belt.

I need some jeans.

I need a pair of pants.

I need socks.

I need a pair of socks.

I need gloves.

I need a pair of gloves.

I need a bathing suit.

I need a swimsuit.

561   When you are just looking and not buying

I'm just browsing.

Thank you, I'm just looking.

Just looking.

562   Choosing merchandise in a store

I just can't make up my mind.

I'm not sure which I like.

Which do you prefer?

563   Questions a customer might ask in a store

Do you have this in blue?

Do you have this in suede?

Do you have this in wool?

Do you have this in a larger size?

Do you have this in a smaller size?

Do you have something a bit less expensive?

Do you have anything less expensive?

Got anything cheaper? (*informal*)

Do you have this in stock?

Do you have any more of these?

Do you have a shirt to match this?

Do you have a shirt to match?

564   When a customer wants to try on clothing

I'd like to try this on.

I want to try this on.

Can I try these on?

Where is the fitting room?

How many items can I take in the dressing room?

565   Encouraging remarks a salesperson might make to a customer

That looks nice on you.

That looks great on you.

That's your color.

This is you!

It's you!

That's you!

That flatters you.

That's very flattering.

That really flatters your figure.

566   **Asking how a purchase will be paid for**

How would you like to pay for this?

How do you want to pay for this?

Would you like to put that on layaway?

> *layaway = a purchase method where a deposit is made and the merchandise is held by the merchant until the balance is paid*

Will that be cash or credit?

Will that be cash or charge?

What method of payment will you use?

567   **When a salesperson cannot supply exactly what is wanted**

We don't have that in your size.

We don't have it in that color.

We're out of that item.

I can back order that for you.

I can issue you a rain check.

568   **When merchandise is not satisfactory**

It's too tight.

It's too loose.

I don't like the color.

I'll have to keep looking for what I want.

It's a little pricey.

> *pricey = expensive*

It's too expensive.

569   **Asking about payment plans in a store**

Is it on sale?

Will it be on sale soon?

Is it going on sale soon?

Can I put it on layaway?

> *layaway = a purchase method where a deposit is made and the merchandise is held by the merchant until the balance is paid*

Can you hold it for me?

Will you hold it for me?

Do you have a layaway plan?

Do you take credit?

Can I apply for a credit card?

570 Getting a purchase gift wrapped in a store

Can I get it gift wrapped?

May I get it gift wrapped?

Can I get this gift wrapped?

Where is the gift-wrap counter?

Is there a charge for gift wrapping?

Can you gift wrap that?

Would you please gift wrap that?

SHOE REPAIR SHOPS

571 Instructions for a shoe repair clerk

I need a shine.

> *I need ≈ I'd like, I want, I would like, Can I have (?)*

I need some new shoelaces.

I need these resoled.

I need the toes widened.

I need a new insert.

I need new heels.

How about some new heels?

What will it cost to have these resoled?

These need shining.

Please polish them, too.

DRUGSTORES

572 **Questions for a pharmacist**

Can I get this prescription filled?

> *Can I get ≈ May I have, Is it possible to get*

Can I get this refilled?

Is this refillable?

Do you need my insurance card?

Do you have my prescription on file?

573 **Requests to a pharmacist for special instructions**

Should I take this with meals?

What happens if I miss taking these pills?

Will this make me drowsy?

Does this (drug) have any side effects?

What are the side effects of this drug?

574 **Requesting general merchandise at a drugstore**

I need some aspirin.

> *I need ≈ I'd like, I'm looking for*

I need some antiseptic.

I need some eye drops.

I need insect repellent.

I need razor blades.

I need film (for my camera).

I need some foot powder.

THE POST OFFICE

575 **A postal clerk greeting a customer**

Next.

Who's next?

Can I help someone?

May I help you?

How may I help you?

How can I help you?

576 **Buying postage stamps**

I need some stamps, please.

I'd like to buy a (first class) stamp, please.

> *I'd like ≈ I want, Can I (?), I need*

I'd like to buy a book of stamps, please.

I'd like to buy a roll of stamps, please.

I'd like to buy a sheet of stamps, please.

577 **Giving instructions to a postal clerk**

This needs to go first class.

First class, please.

Air mail, please.

I need this to go express mail.

> *I need ≈ I want, I'd like, I would like*

I need to send this overnight.

I need to send this second-day mail.

I need to send this parcel post.

I need to send this by certified mail.

I need to send this by registered mail.

Return receipt requested, please.

578 **Asking questions at a post office**

How much postage do I need for this?

How much postage does this need?

How much postage do I need to send this air mail?

Can you weigh this?

How do I get my mail forwarded?

Do you have any envelopes I could buy?

How long will it take (to get there)?

Can I have the ZIP code for Chicago?

May I have the ZIP code for Chicago?

Would you give me the ZIP code for Chicago?
Can I have a change-of-address form?
Can I rent a post office box?
Do you have any tax forms?
Can I pick up a package?
I'd like to pick up a package.
Will you please hold my mail?

579 **Questions a postal clerk might ask a customer**
First class?
How many stamps do you need?
A sheet or a roll (of stamps)?
How many?
Any particular style?

580 **Miscellaneous expressions used by a postal clerk**
We're (all) out of those.
That should arrive on Monday.
That ought to arrive on Monday.
Let's hope that arrives on Monday.
Sorry, you will have to stand in line.
Sorry, you will have to take a place in line.
Please print legibly.
Can I see some ID?

> *ID = identification*

I'll have to see some ID.
Please show me your driver's license.
I'm sorry, I can only release the package to the person it
is addressed to.
The forms are over there.
Please fill out a form and bring it back to me.

581 **A postal clerk bringing a transaction to an end**
Would you like anything else?

Do you need anything else (today)?
Anything else?
Will that be all?
Is that all?

THE TAILOR

582   Questions asked of a tailor

Do you do alterations on men's clothing?
Do you do alterations on women's clothing?
Do you do reweaving?
Can you repair a tear in leather?
What options do I have for fabric?
Can you match this color?

583   Giving instructions to a tailor

This needs to be hemmed.
This needs hemming.
The hem needs to be raised an inch.
The hem needs to be let down.
The pants legs need to be let down.
The waist needs a few tucks.
The waist needs to be taken in an inch.
The waist needs to be let out.
This jacket is tight under the arms.
It's too short in the sleeves.
The sleeves are too long.

TICKETS

584   Requests made to a ticket agent

I'd like four seats for tonight, please.
Do you have four seats for tonight, please?
Where are the best seats you have left?

Do you have anything in the first four rows?
Do you have matinees?
How much are the tickets?
Can I exchange these for another night?
Is it possible to exchange these for another night?

585   Asking questions about payment for tickets
Do you have senior citizen discounts?
Do you have student rates?
Do you have group rates?
Do you take checks?
Do you take credit cards?
Which credit cards do you take?

586   Asking questions about an entertainment event
How long does the show run?
When does the show close?
Is there an intermission?
Where are the rest rooms?
Do you sell concessions?
How soon does the curtain go up?
What time does the curtain go up?
When does the curtain go up?

587   Questions asked by a ticket agent for an entertainment event
Did you make a reservation?
Do you have reservations?
Do you have a reservation?
What name did you reserve the tickets under?

588   Expressions about tickets to an entertainment event
I'm sorry, these tickets are nonrefundable.
I'm sorry, there are no tickets available.

I'm sorry, we're sold out tonight.

That performance is sold out.

I'm sorry, at fifteen minutes before curtain time we release
unclaimed tickets to the waiting list.

> *curtain time = the beginning of the performance*

The house is full. I can put you on the waiting list.

Would you care to make a reservation for another night?

Do you want to make a reservation for another night?

Would you like to make a reservation for another night?

Do you want reservations for any other night?

589   Payment for an entertainment event

The tickets are $7.50 plus tax.

Students and seniors are $2 off.

> *seniors = people over sixty-five*

I'm running out of change; do you have (any) smaller
bills?

Do you have anything smaller?

Do you have anything smaller than that?

590   Information about an entertainment event

There is an intermission.

The show runs about two hours.

The house opens in about five minutes.

Please be seated. The show begins soon.

The coat room is around the corner, if you'd like to check
your coat.

The concession stand is over there, if you'd care for
something.

> *concession stand = a wagon or counter where
> refreshments and souvenirs are sold*

The usher will give you your program.

There is no seating after the house lights are dimmed.

You will have to wait for the intermission to be seated.

FLORISTS

591   Ordering flowers from a florist

I'd like a dozen roses, please.

    I'd like ≈ I need, I'm looking for, I want

I'd like a corsage, please.

I'd like a floral arrangement.

I'd like an arrangement.

I'd like some flowers for my wife.

What kinds of vases do you have?

What do you have in season?

Which flowers are the freshest?

Do you deliver?

Can you deliver this to the hospital?

Would it be possible to deliver this to the hospital today?

How far do you deliver?

What are your delivery charges?

592   Questions a florist might ask a customer

May I help you?

What kind of flowers did you have in mind?

Short stemmed or long stemmed?

What color did you want?

Vase or wrapped?

Did you want those delivered?

Should I send them directly to the funeral home?

What do you want the card to say?

NEWSPAPERS AND MAGAZINES

593   Requesting a publication from a news vendor

Morning edition, please.

City edition.

Evening edition.

Sports final.

Do you carry *The Wall Street Journal?*
Do you stock *Time* magazine?
When is the next issue out?

594 Requesting a subscription from a magazine agent

I'd like to subscribe.

> *I'd like ≈ I want, I would like*

I'd like a subscription.
I'd like a two-year subscription at the reduced rate.
I'd like to renew my subscription.
I'd like to change my subscription to weekends only.
I'd like to cancel my subscription.
I'd like to take advantage of your special offer for new subscribers.
Give me a subscription to *Time.*

595 Making a complaint to a newspaper agent

I didn't receive a newspaper this morning.
I didn't get a paper today.
I didn't get today's paper.
The delivery person threw my paper in the ditch.
They always throw my paper in the neighbor's yard.
My paper has been arriving late.
My paper was missing the comics section this morning.

596 Expressions used with a newspaper agent

Can you leave the paper on the porch?
I'm going on vacation. Can you hold my paper for two weeks?

> *hold my paper = stop delivery of my paper*

I'm moving, and I'd like to give you my new address.
I'd like to order a back issue.
I received a past-due notice.
Bill me.

597 Responses from a magazine agent

May I have your name and address?

Give me your name and address.

May I have your ZIP code?

What's the ZIP code there?

Would you like a six-month or one-year subscription?

May I ask why you wish to cancel?

Thank you for your order.

598 A newspaper agent responding to complaints

I apologize for the inconvenience.

I'm sorry for the inconvenience.

I'm terribly sorry about that.

We'll have a paper sent out to you right away.

I'll send out the missing issue right away.

I'll make sure the matter is taken care of.

AUTOMOBILES

599 An automobile dealer greeting a customer

Hello, can I help you?

Can I help you with something?

Can I show you something?

What were you looking for?

Do you need any help?

600 An automobile dealer finding out what you want

This model is available with automatic transmission.

This is a very popular model.

If you want comfort, this one is for you.

Do you prefer four doors or two?

Were you looking for something in a new car or a used
    one?

601   **Choosing a car**

I need a new car.

> *I need ≈ I'd like, I'm looking for, I'm in the market for, What do you have in (?)*

I need a used car.

I need a station wagon.

I need a van.

I need a mini-van.

I need a used car with an air bag.

I need a (good) used car.

I need an economy car.

I need a sports car.

I need a four-door.

I need an American-made car.

I'm just looking, thanks.

> *(a formula for telling a salesperson that you are not ready to buy anything)*

602   **Choosing a new car's options**

I need a car with air-conditioning.

> *I need ≈ I'd like, I'm looking for, I'm in the market for, I want, I have to have*

I need air-conditioning.

I need automatic door locks.

I need power steering and power brakes.

I need automatic transmission.

I need four-wheel drive.

I might want the anti-lock braking system.

Is it stick shift or automatic?

> *stick shift = standard transmission*

What are the standard features?

What comes on it?

What's standard?

What safety features does it have?

What sort of mileage does this car get?

What sort of mileage does this thing get? (*informal*)

Does this car get good mileage?

What about mileage?

What would you suggest?

603 Concerning the price of a car

What's the sticker price?

> *the sticker price = the manufacturer's suggested retail price*

What are you asking for it?

How much are you asking for it?

What's the asking price?

Hey, I'm not made of money! (*informal*)

Are you willing to negotiate?

Come on! You'll never sell it at that price! (*informal*)

That's my last offer. Take it or leave it. (*cliché*)

What do you have for $3,000?

What d'ya got for $3,000? (*informal*)

604 Financing a car

I'll need financing.

I'll have to have financing.

I need to arrange financing.

Do you offer bank financing?

What is the lowest possible interest rate you have?

Can you get me a good deal on a loan?

605 Test-driving a car

Can I take **her** for a spin? (*informal*)

> *her = the car*

Can I take it for a spin? (*informal*)

> *a spin = a drive*

Can I take it for a test drive?
Will you let me take it for a test drive?
I'd like to take it for a test drive.
Can I take it for a road test?
Let's give it a road test.
Let's see what it'll do on the highway.
What'll this baby do on the highway? (*informal*)

BABYSITTERS

606 Arranging for a babysitter

Can you babysit for us next Friday night?

> *Can you ≈ Will you, Would you, Would you be able to,*
> *Are you able to*

Can you drive over?

Can you sit for three children?

We will pick you up at eight.

We have two children. How much do you charge?

Have you ever babysat for an infant?

607 Basic instructions to a babysitter

No guests while we're gone.

No visitors while we're gone.

Could you clean up a little, too?

Please read to the kids before they go to bed.

We'll be home by midnight.

Keep all the doors locked.

Please don't tie up the telephone for long periods.

If anyone calls, please take a message.

We will call later to check (on the kids).

Do you have any questions?

608 Telling a babysitter how to reach you

Here's the phone number where we'll be.

Here are the emergency numbers.

Here's the number where you can reach us.

Here's where you can reach us.

609   **When a babysitter gets hungry**

There's food in the fridge.

Help yourself to anything in the fridge.

Help yourself to a snack.

Please don't eat the last piece of pie.

610   **Questions a babysitter might ask**

Where will you be?

Where can you be reached?

Can you leave me the number where you'll be?

   Can you ≈ Will you, Would you

Who do I call in case of emergency?

How late will you be?

How late will you be out?

What time will you be coming home?

Do I have to feed them?

Do they get any medicine?

What time do the kids go to bed?

When's their bedtime?

Where are their pajamas?

Can I have a friend over?

   Can I ≈ May I, Do you mind if I, Is it okay if I

611   **Instructions to a babysitter about feeding and bedtime**

Give the kids dinner at six.

Timmy is allergic to orange juice.

No snacks before bedtime.

Please give Jimmy his medicine at bedtime.

Make sure the kids are in bed by 8:00.

Have the kids in bed by 8:00.

Put the kids to bed at 8:00.

Bedtime is 8:00.

612   **Financial arrangements with a babysitter**
I charge by the hour.
My rate is $5.50 per hour.
I charge standard rates.
I charge more for more than one child.

613   **When the parents return**
Is everything all right?
How were the children?
Were there any problems?
Were there any telephone calls?
Did the children behave?
What time did they get to bed?

COMPUTER REPAIR

614   **Stating what's wrong with a computer**
I can't get it to work.
I'm using the keyboard but nothing's happening.
Nothing happens.
I can't log on.
> *to log on = to start a computer session*

I can't log in.
> *to log in = to start a computer session*

I can't access the menu.
I can't access my disc.
> *disc = hard or floppy disc storage medium*

It says I have a bad disc sector.
My disc is fried. (*slang*)
> *fried = burned out (in this context)*

The screen is blank.
The monitor is blank.

The monitor is wavy.

The screen is frozen.

frozen = not moving

It crashed. (*slang*)

crashed = ceased to function (in this context)

It keeps crashing. (*slang*)

I can't get into the program.

I can't get into my file.

I don't remember the password.

615   Asking about computer operation

How do I get back to the disc operating system?

How do I get back to DOS?

DOS = disc operating system

How do I get back to the main menu?

How do I pull up the menu?

How do I print out a file?

How do I get it to print?

How do I get it to print out?

My document isn't printing right.

How do I get my document out of the print queue?

the print queue = the sequence of files waiting to be printed

How do I initialize my printer?

to initialize = to set up electronically

My disc is full.

How do you format discs?

to format = to prepare for receiving data (in this context)

What does 'incompatible file format' mean?

How do I change fonts?

How do I change the paper orientation?

CLOTHES CLEANING

616 Placing an order with a dry cleaner or a launderer

Can you get this stain out?

Is it possible to get a stain like this out?

I'd like to have this pressed, please.

These need to be laundered.

This needs dry cleaning.

Can you remove this stain without harming the fabric?

Can you repair this tear?

Can you fix this zipper?

How much will a new zipper cost?

I need this by tomorrow.

No starch, please.

A button is missing.

All the buttons were there when I brought it in.

I'm sorry, I lost my ticket.

I'm sorry, I forgot my ticket.

617 A dry cleaner or launderer offering services

(Any) starch?

Do you want starch?

Do you want starch (in these shirts)?

Do you want me to repair that tear?

I can put on a new button, but it may not match exactly.

Is Tuesday OK?

> = *Is it all right that your clothes will be ready Tuesday?*

We are not responsible for missing buttons.

Do you have your receipt?

Your ticket, please.

There is a charge for replacing buttons.

618 Making a complaint to a dry cleaner or launderer

This garment is simply not clean.

You have shrunk my jacket!

There is way too much starch in these shirts.

There is a tear in the fabric that wasn't there when I
brought this in.

You tore my dress.

The fabric appears to be damaged.

**619   A dry cleaner or a launderer offering responses to
complaints**

The dress was torn when we first saw it.

That spot cannot be removed.

I warned you that the fabric was too delicate for cleaning.

I cannot give you this garment without some
identification.

PUBLIC LIBRARIES

620   Questions for a librarian

Where is the reference section?

Where is the fiction?

Can you please tell me where to find the biographies?

Where are the periodicals?

periodicals = magazines and journals

Where can I get a library card?

Do you have a photocopier here?

Is there a quiet reading room?

Do you check out video cassettes?

Do you have CDs available?

CD = compact disc

Where is the public telephone?

621   At the service counter of a library

I'd like to check out these books.

I'd like to check these books out.

These books are overdue.

overdue = late

I'd like to return these books.

I need to pay a fine.

Do you have change for the copiers?

622   A library desk clerk's responses

The copier is in the reference room.

Please ask the adult services librarian about CDs.

The periodical room is upstairs.

The telephones are in the lobby.

This book is due in three weeks.

Reference books cannot be checked out.

Would you like me to reserve this book for you?

> *Would you like me to ≈ Shall I, Should I, Do you want me to*

Would you like me to request this book from another library?

This book is overdue.

THE LIFEGUARD

623   Questions for a lifeguard

How far out can we swim?

How deep is it by the raft?

Is there a steep drop-off?

When does the tide come in?

Is the current strong?

Is there an undertow?

Is there an undercurrent?

What time does the beach close?

624   A lifeguard's instructions to swimmers

Don't swim past the buoys.

Watch out for the undertow.

No horseplay.

> *horseplay = rough or dangerous play*

No running on the deck!

No glass bottles or drinking glasses allowed around the pool.

The beach is closed today.

The beach is closing; come out of the water.

Get out of the water.

PLUMBING PROBLEMS

625   **Describing plumbing problems — sinks**

My sink is clogged.

My sink is backed up.

My sink isn't draining properly.

My kitchen sink is full of yuck. (*slang*)

> *yuck = nasty matter; grease and garbage*

626   **Describing plumbing problems — toilets**

The toilet is running.

The toilet won't stop running.

The toilet runs until I jiggle the handle.

The toilet won't flush.

The toilet is leaking.

My toilet overflowed!

627   **Describing plumbing problems — bathtubs**

The tub is leaking.

The bathtub is backing up.

> *= Water is coming into the tub through the waste pipes.*

The sewer is backed up.

> *= Sewage is flowing in instead of out.*

The sump pump isn't working.

My bathroom is flooded.

The tub faucets leak day and night.

628 **Describing plumbing problems — water pipes**
My pipes are rusty.
The water is discolored.
The water is rust-colored.
The pipes are always banging.

629 **Describing plumbing problems — water heater**
The hot water heater's out.
The hot water heater is leaking.
I don't have any hot water.
The water heater keeps going out.
There is never any flame in the water heater.
The water is never hot enough.
The water is too hot.

UTILITY SERVICE

630 **Requesting service from a utility company by telephone**
I need to set up service.
> *I need ≈ I want, I'd like, I would like, I have, I'm calling*

I need to establish service.
I need to disconnect service.
I need to change the name on the bill.
I need to change the billing address.
I need to change my account to another address.
I have a problem with my bill.

631 **Reporting problems to a utility company**
I received a notice that someone stopped by to get a meter reading.
My lights keep flickering.
My water pressure is very low.
I smell gas.

My electricity was cut off.

My gas was cut off.

We have a power outage almost every week.

The meter reader never waits long enough for me to get to the door.

HAIR CARE

632   Requests and inquiries to a barber or hairdresser

Shampoo and blow dry, please.

I'd like my hair dyed.

> *I'd like ≈ I need, I want*

I'd like a permanent.

I'd like a perm.

I'd like just a trim.

How much is a perm?

Do I have to have an appointment to get a haircut?

Just a trim, please.

Just trim off the ends.

Can you touch up the gray?

I wear my part to the left.

I part my hair on the left.

I part my hair in the middle.

Could I make an appointment for next month?

633   Requesting a man's haircut

Trim around the ears, please.

A little off the sides.

I'm letting my sideburns grow.

I'd like a shave, please.

Trim my beard and mustache, please.

See what you can do with this head of hair. (*informal*)

Leave it long.

Tapered in the back.

I'd like it spiky on top.
Could you take a little more off the top?

> *Could you ≈ Will you, Would you please*

Could you take a little more off in back?
Could you take a little more off the sides?

634 Responses from a barber or hairdresser

Sorry, you have to have an appointment.
Sit right down. No appointment necessary.
What would you like?
Are you going for a particular look?
Shampoo and rinse?
What color were you thinking about?
Step over to the dryers.
How does that look?
How's that?
Would you like to schedule your next appointment?
When would you like your next appointment?

635 A barber or hairdresser asking about a man's haircut

How much do you want me to take off?
Do you want it tapered in the back?
How much do you want cut off?
How much do you want off?
Shall I shave your outline?

636 A barber or hairdresser giving instructions to the client

Please turn your head to the right.
Look down.
Don't move so much.
Hold still.

637   A barber or hairdresser asking for payment
That will be nine dollars.
Nine dollars, please.
Twelve dollars, since this is the weekend.

638   Payment to a barber or a hairdresser
What do I owe you?
How much do I owe you?
How much is it?

DOMESTIC HELP

639   Praising a house-cleaner
Everything looks very nice.
Everything is clean.
Everything is fine.
The kitchen looks lovely.
(It) looks good.
(It) looks great!
You do such nice work.

640   Instructions for a house-cleaner
There are cobwebs in the corners.
You need to dust more carefully.
There is lint up next to the wall.
The bathtub needs scrubbing.
Please vacuum and dust the whole house.
Please wash the floors.
Please scrub the floors.
Do not use abrasive cleanser on the bathroom sink.
Please wax the kitchen floor.
Make sure the drapes hang straight when you finish.
Make sure you vacuum the throw rugs.

641   House-cleaner to employer

Is everything all right?

I hope everything is satisfactory.

I need more cleaner.

I need more furniture polish.

I need more plastic garbage bags.

642   Employer to lawn-care worker

It looks very nice.

The lawn looks lovely.

Everything is fine.

The place looks good enough to live in. (*jocular*)

The place looks nice enough to live in. (*jocular*)

You did a good job.

643   Instructions to lawn-care worker

Please water the grass.

The grass needs to be cut shorter.

Do not cut the grass so short.

Sweep the clippings from the driveway.

Place the clippings in the plastic bags.

Place the clippings in the large paper bags.

Place the bags at the curb.

Please trim more carefully.

The shrubbery needs trimming.

Please edge around the shrubbery.

Please edge the sidewalks and driveway.

Do not damage the base of the trees with the mower.

Be careful around the rosebushes.

We are going to have to do something about these weeds.

You need to spray the weeds.

It is time to fertilize the lawn.

Please spread fertilizer on the lawn.

644   Lawn-care worker to employer
Should I trim the bushes this time?
How do things look?
Do you want me to edge?
Do you want me to fertilize?
Shall I treat the lawn for weeds?

TELEPHONES

ANSWERING THE TELEPHONE

645   Answering the telephone — residential

Hello.

Smith residence.

Hello, Smith residence.

Yo! (*informal*)

Yeah! (*informal*)

Yes.

John Jones.

Hello, this is John Jones (speaking).

John Jones, may I help you?

John.

John, may I help you?

646   Answering the telephone — business

City Hall. What department please?

Smith Company.

Smith Company, may I help you?

Smithco, how may I direct your call?

647   Asking whom a telephone caller wants to talk to

Who do you want to talk to?

Who do you want to speak with?

Who do you wish to speak to?

Whom do you wish to speak to?

With whom do you wish to speak? (*formal*)

648   Screening someone's telephone calls

May I tell her who's calling?

May I ask who is calling?

Whom may I say is calling? (*formal*)

Who shall I say is calling?

Whom shall I say is calling? (*formal*)

Who's calling?

Is she expecting your call?

649 Connecting or transferring a telephone caller

Do you wish me to page Mrs. Robins?

I will see if she's in the building.

Let me page her.

Let me connect you with that department.

650 Putting a telephone caller on hold

He is on another line. Will you hold?

Would you care to hold? (*formal*)

Would you like to hold?

Just a moment, please.

Please hold.

Hold, please.

Hold the line. (*informal*)

Can you hold?

651 Interrupting a telephone call with other business

Just a moment, I have another call.

Hang on a moment.

> *to hang on = to wait*

Hang on a sec(ond).

652 Taking a call off hold

For whom are you holding? (*formal*)

Whom are you holding for? (*formal*)

Who are you holding for?

Who's on the line?

Are you being helped?

Have you been helped?

May I help you?

Can I help you?

653 Offering to take a message from a telephone caller

He's not in; would you like to call back?

She is not available. Can I take a message?

She is away from her desk. Can I take a message?

May I take a message? (*formal*)

Could I take a message?

Could I have someone call you?

654 Offering to help a telephone caller

Is there anyone else who could help you?

I would be happy to try to answer your question.

Would you care to talk to her secretary?

Could I help you?

655 Bringing a telephone call to an end

I have to get back to work before the boss sees me.

I have to get back to my work. I will call again later.

There's someone on the other line. I must say good-bye now.

I really have to go now.

I'll have to take your number and call you back.

Can I call you back? Something has come up.

Can we continue this later? My other line is ringing.

The doorbell is ringing. I'll call you back.

TELEPHONE SERVICE

656 Requesting a telephone number from directory assistance

I'd like the number for Dr. Pat Smith on Main Street.

I need the number for Dr. Pat Smith on Main Street.

Can you give me the number for Dr. Pat Smith on Main Street?

What is the area code for Los Angeles?

I need the area code for Los Angeles.

657   **Requests to a telephone operator**

I can't get through to this number. Would you dial it for me?

Could you help me place a call?

I'd like to make a collect call.

I'd like this billed to my home number.

I'd like to place a person-to-person call.

Can you put me through to Chicago?

Could you dial it for me, please?

658   **Making emergency calls**

I want to report a fire.

I want to report a robbery in progress.

There is a house on fire at 406 Maple Street.

There's been an accident and we need an ambulance.

This is an emergency.

I need the police.

Please connect me with the police.

Get me the police and hurry.

659   **Making complaints about unwanted telephone calls**

I've been getting prank calls.

     prank = joke

I've been getting crank calls.

     crank = bothersome; harassing

I've been getting harassing calls.

I've been getting obscene phone calls.

660 Describing problems with a pay telephone

This telephone may be out of order.

I'm trying to use my calling card, but I'm not getting through.

The phone ate my money. (*jocular*)

This phone won't take any more money.

661 Requesting telephone service or installation

I'd like to order service.

I'd like to order a second line.

I'd like to get call waiting.

I'd like to get touch-tone dialing.

I need new phone jacks installed.

I'm moving and I need a new number.

I'd like a private listing.

I'd like an unlisted number.

I need to speak with someone about my bill.

662 Expressions used by a telephone directory assistance operator

What city, please?

City, please?

Name, please?

Hold for the number, please.

Business or residence?

Is this a business or residence?

I'm sorry, you have the wrong area code.

I'm sorry, that's an unlisted number.

I'm sorry, that number is nonpublished.

I'm sorry, at the customer's request, that number is not published.

I'm sorry, I don't have a listing under that name.

I'm not showing a listing.

There is no listing under that spelling.

Are you sure of the spelling?

How is that spelled?

On what street?

Do you have an address?

663 Expressions used by a telephone repair service operator

It sounds like a problem with our lines.

It sounds like a problem in your house wiring.

There is a charge if the problem is with the wiring inside your house.

I can have a repair person come out tomorrow.

Let me connect you with my supervisor.

664 Expressions used by a telephone company sales representative

Would you care for any other services?

Would you be interested in call waiting?

When would you like the phone number changed?

665 Recorded telephone service messages

The number you have dialed, 555-1234, has been changed. The new number is 555-1235. Please make a note of it.

The number you have dialed, 555-1234, has been disconnected.

The number you have dialed, 555-1234, is not in service.

No further information is available on 555-1234.

555-1234 has been temporarily disconnected.

555-1234 is temporarily out of service.

555-1234 is being checked for trouble.

All circuits are busy now.

Please try again later.

That number is busy, please try again later.

When making a call outside of your area code, please dial 1.

The area code of the number you have dialed has been changed to 555.

Your call cannot be completed as dialed. Please check the number and try again.

SHOPPING ON THE TELEPHONE

666 **Asking about store hours over the telephone**

What time do you open?

When do you open?

When are you open?

What are your hours?

When do you close today?

How late are you open (today)?

Are you open on weekends?

Are you open on Saturday?

Are you open after five?

667 **Asking about the location of some place**

Where are you located?

What are the (nearest) cross streets?

Where is your store?

What's your nearest location?

Do you have any locations in the suburbs?

What mall are you in?

How do I get there?

668 **Asking how to place a merchandise order over the telephone**

Do you have a catalog?

I'd like to place an order.

Can I fax my order in?

Can I fax my order to you?

669 Asking about payment for goods ordered over the telephone

Do you accept credit cards?

Which credit cards do you take?

Do you take credit?

Do you take checks?

Do you accept checks?

TELEPHONE SOLICITATION

670 When you are interrupted by a telephone solicitor

I'm sorry, but I'm not interested.

I don't have time to talk right now.

I can't talk right now.

You caught me in the middle of dinner.

How did you get my name?

No, thank you.

We do not accept telephone solicitations.

671 Requesting additional information from a telephone solicitor

Can you send me some information in writing?

Can you send me some literature?

Can you send me a catalog?

Can you send me a brochure?

672 Refusing to do business with a telephone solicitor

I'm sorry, I don't give out my credit card number over the phone.

I'm sorry, but I don't place orders over the phone.

I never do business with telephone solicitors.

Please take me off your list!

TRAVEL AND
TRANSPORTATION

TRAVEL AGENTS

673 Questions asked by a travel agent

Where would you like to go?

When would you like to go?

What days would you like to travel?

Where to?

One-way or round-trip?

Any particular airline?

Smoking or nonsmoking?

Smoking or non?

Aisle or window seat?

Are you a member of the frequent flyer program?

How would you like to pay for your tickets?

674 Requests made to a travel agent

I'd like to book a cruise.

What ports of call does the ship stop in?

Which ships stop at Barbados?

Which ships call at Barbados?

I'd like to book a flight.

I need tickets to Chicago.

I'd like a round-trip ticket to New York, please.

I'd like a one-way ticket to Los Angeles.

I'd like a window seat.

I'd like an aisle seat.

I'd like a no-smoking flight.

Are all flights nonsmoking?

I need to leave in the morning.

I need to return on Saturday.

Can you sign me up for a frequent flyer program?

675   Questions about the cost of travel

How much is coach?

>   coach = tourist class

How much is first class?

How much is business class?

How many weeks in advance do I have to buy to get a discount?

Is there a discount for a 14-day advance purchase?

Do I have to stay over Saturday night?

Would it be cheaper if I left on Thursday, instead?

AIR TRAVEL

676   Questions a passenger might ask about an airline flight

Is it direct?

Is it nonstop?

Is there a layover?

How long is the layover?

Do I have to change planes?

Is a meal served?

Is there a meal?

Can I order a special meal?

Do you have my frequent flyer number?

How much carry-on luggage is permitted?

How many items of carry-on luggage are permitted?

How much carry-on luggage am I allowed?

How much luggage can I carry on?

677   Describing types of airline flights

It's nonstop.

You'll change planes in Denver.

You have a layover in Chicago.

There's a one-hour layover in Dallas.

You only have 20 minutes to make your connection.

All domestic flights are nonsmoking.

A lunch will be served in flight.

A snack will be served in flight.

There is no meal service on this flight.

There is nothing to eat on this flight.

These tickets are nonrefundable.

That fare requires a 14-day advance purchase.

To be eligible for the lower fare, you have to stay over a Saturday night.

I'm sorry, that flight is booked.

You could try going standby.

The State Department has issued a travel warning in that area.

678　Questions a passenger might ask of an airline ticket agent

When does the next flight leave?

Can I get onto the next flight?

Are there seats still available?

Are there tickets available on standby?

Can I go standby?

Is the plane on time?

What's the departure time?

When does the plane get here?

What's the arrival time?

Will I be able to make my connection?

Will they hold my connecting flight?

679　Rescheduling an airline flight

I need to cancel my flight.

I need to reschedule my flight.

Can I change my flight schedule?

Can I change my itinerary?

Is there a penalty for changing my plans?

680 Complaining about lost or damaged luggage

My luggage is missing.

One of my bags seems to be missing.

You lost my luggage! (*informal*)

My luggage is damaged.

Can you check to see where my luggage is?

681 Asking about frequent flyer mileage

Are you in our frequent flyer program?

Would you like to sign up for our frequent flyer program?

Do you know how our frequent flyer program works?

Do you have your frequent flyer number?

Would you like to use your frequent flyer miles?

Would you like to sign up in our frequent flyer program?

682 Announcing changes in an airline flight

This flight has been delayed.

This flight has been delayed due to bad weather.

This flight has been delayed; however, all connecting
  flights can be made.

This flight has been cancelled.

This flight has been moved to gate K1.

683 When an airplane is crowded

We have a very full flight this evening.

This flight is overbooked.

Would anyone be interested in giving up their seat in
  exchange for a free ticket?

684 **At the airport boarding gate**

We will begin boarding soon.

At this time we'd like to pre-board those passengers with young children or those needing extra assistance.

We would now like to begin general boarding.

We are now boarding passengers in rows 24 through 36.

We are now boarding all rows on Flight 1234 to Columbus.

May I see your boarding pass?

You're permitted two carry-on items.

You may only carry on one item of luggage.

You'll have to check that item of luggage.

You'll have to check your other bag.

685 **On an airplane**

You're in seat 12F.

You're in my seat.

Please observe the no smoking signs.

The emergency exits are located on either side of the plane over the wings.

Please bring your attention to the center aisle as the flight attendants explain the safety rules.

To fasten your seat belt bring the two ends together, and to release the seat belt pull up on the latch.

In the unlikely event of a water landing, your seat cushion may be used as a flotation device.

Please locate the exit nearest you.

Please keep your seat belts fastened until the captain has turned off the seat belt sign.

Please remain in your seat until the plane has come to a complete stop.

The captain has turned on the fasten seat belts sign.

Please return to your seat.

Please bring your seat back to its full upright position.

686   Eating and drinking on an airplane
What would you like to drink?
Would you care for some nuts?
Nuts?
Thank you for flying American Airlines.
Are you having dinner this evening?
Will you be having lunch today?
Can I offer you a snack?
Would you like the chicken or the beef (entree)?
Coffee or tea?
Would you like coffee?
Coffee?

687   Entering the United States through customs and immigration
Do you have anything to declare?
Did you buy anything?
Are you bringing anything into the country with you?
How much currency are you bringing into the country?
May I see your passport?
Do you have your visa?
What is your citizenship?
How long were you out of the country?
How long do you plan on staying?
What is the purpose of your visit?
What was the nature of your trip?
Please place your suitcases on the table.
I need to examine the contents of your purse.

RAILWAY TRAVEL

688   Instructions from a commuter train conductor
Stand clear of the doors.
Please move away from the doors.

For your safety, don't lean on the doors.

No smoking, littering, or radio playing.

Please have your tickets ready for the conductor.

Next stop is St. Louis.

Next stop, Galesburg.

Omaha is next.

Trains are immediately following.

Step up.

689   Asking about a long train trip

Is it direct?

Is there a layover?

How long is the layover?

Do I have to change trains?

Is there a dining car?

Can I order a special meal?

Can I check my baggage through?

   through = all the way to my destination

How much luggage can I carry on?

When does the next train leave?

Are there seats still available?

Is the train on time?

What's the departure time?

When does the train get in?

What's the arrival time?

690   Asking about a train seat you want to sit in

Is anyone sitting here?

Anyone sitting here?

Would you mind moving your things?

Is this seat taken?

Is this seat occupied?

Is this space taken?

Could I sit here?

Can I have this seat?

May I have your seat (when you leave)?

691   Making requests on a train

Move over. (*informal*)

Could you move your stuff?

Can you open the window?

Can you close the window?

Can you crack the window?

> *crack the window = open the window slightly*

692   Asking questions on a train

Where are we?

What stop are we at?

Where is Grand Avenue?

Can you let me know when we get to Evanston?

How far are we from the center of town?

How many more stops before we reach the end of the line?

> *the end of the line = the last stop on the route*

What stop is next?

Is this where I get off?

How long will it take to get to Chicago?

LONG-DISTANCE BUS TRAVEL

693   Asking about a long bus trip

Is it direct?

Is there a layover?

How long is the layover?

Do I have to change buses?

Do we stop for meals?

Can I check my baggage through?

> *through = all the way to my destination*

How much luggage can I carry on?

When does the next bus leave?

Can I reserve a seat (in advance)?

Is the bus on time?

What's the departure time?

When does the bus get in?

694   Asking about a bus seat you want to sit in

Is anyone sitting here?

Is this seat taken?

Is this space taken? (*formal*)

Is this seat occupied? (*formal*)

LOCAL BUS AND SUBWAY TRAVEL

695   Asking about bus and subway fare

What is the fare?

How much is the fare?

How much?

696   General questions when boarding a bus

Could I have a transfer, please?

> *a transfer = a slip of paper that allows the rider to continue the journey on another bus without paying the full fare again*

Transfer, please.

Is this the right bus for Main Street?

Does this bus go downtown?

697   Asking about bus routes

How far does this bus go?

Is this the bus to Linden Avenue?

Does this bus go to Howard Street?

Could you let me know when we get to Davis Street?

Can you tell me where to get off?

698 **Asking about subway routes**

Which line goes downtown?

line = route; set of subway tracks

Where do I change (trains)?

Is it far to the last stop?

Does the conductor announce the stops?

699 **Making requests on a bus**

Please move over.

Could you move your stuff, please? (*informal*)

Can you open that window?

Can you close the window?

Can you crack the window?

crack the window = open the window slightly

700 **Asking questions on a bus**

Where are we?

What stop are we at?

Where is Grand Avenue?

Can you let me know when we get to Evanston?

How far are we from the center of town?

How many more stops before we reach the end of the line?

What stop is next?

Is this where I should get off?

How long will it take to get to town?

701 **Giving instructions to bus passengers**

Could you please move to the rear?

Move back, please.

Move to the rear, please.

There's plenty of room in back.

702 **Instructions when boarding a bus**

Step up, please.

Watch your step.

I cannot make change.

> *(In some cities drivers do not handle any money.)*

You must have the correct change.

Do you want a transfer?

This transfer has expired.

Step behind the line.

Move to the rear(, please).

There's plenty of room in the rear.

Another quarter, please.

Keep your arms and head inside the bus.

Please exit through the rear door.

> *(The front door is used for boarding and the back door for exiting.)*

Rear door, please.

TAXICABS

703 **Basic instructions to a cab driver**

Take me to the airport.

I need to go to Fifth and Main.

Fifth and Main, please.

704 **A taxi driver asking where to go**

Where to?

Where to, friend?

Where to, chief? *(informal)*

Where to, Bud? *(informal)*

Where to, lady?

What intersection is that near?

(Just) where is that?

Which airport?

705 A taxi driver asking general questions

You in a hurry?

Which way do you want me to go?

I don't go there.

It's rush hour, I don't go to the airport.

I'm not on duty.

Is the radio too loud?

It will cost you double fare to leave the city.

Mind if I smoke?

I'm going to smoke.

Please don't smoke.

706 A taxi driver identifying the final destination

Which corner?

Which side of the street?

Which side of the intersection?

Want me to drop you at the door?

That house (over) there?

Is here okay?

707 Concerning speed in a taxi

To the airport, and be quick about it.

The airport and make it quick.

There's an extra ten in it for you if you can get me there
in ten minutes.

I'm late; please hurry.

Slow down!

Do you have to drive this fast?

There is no need to hurry.

Please drive safely.

708 Concerning smoking in a taxi

Is smoking allowed?

Mind if I smoke?

May I smoke?

I'm allergic to smoke.

I'd prefer that you not smoke. (*formal*)

709 Concerning the temperature in a taxi

It's too cold in here.

It's too hot in here.

Could you turn the heat up?

Could you turn off the air-conditioning?

Please roll up your window.

710 Asking a taxi driver to wait

Please wait here.

Stay here a moment.

Wait here a minute.

Wait here a sec.

711 Paying a taxi fare

Do you have change for a twenty?

Can you break a twenty?

All I have is a twenty.

Keep the change.

I need a receipt.

Give me a receipt.

712 A taxi driver discussing payment

Do you have smaller bills?

Don't you have anything smaller?

I can't break that.

  to break = to make change for

I'm sorry; I don't have (any) change.

Do you need a receipt?

GENERAL TRAVEL

713   When you are lost

Can you help me? I'm lost.

I seem to be lost.

I can't find my way to San José.

714   Verifying your route when traveling

Is this the road to Dallas?

How do I get to Dallas from here?

Am I going north?

Am I headed toward town?

Is the railroad station in this direction?

Which way is north?

How far away is it?

Can I walk there from here?

Could you show me on the map?

Which way is downtown?

Is it far from here?

715   Asking for directions to a specific place

Do you know where 406 Maple Street is?

Do you know where I could find the train station?

Where is the nearest train station?

Where is the nearest bus station?

Where is the freeway?

  freeway ≈ expressway, trafficway, thruway, highway

Where is the post office?

Where can I park?

Is there a parking garage near here?

Is there a drugstore nearby?

Do you know how to find 406 Maple Street?

What's the quickest way to Maple Street?

How do I get to the airport?

How do I get to the train station?

How do I get downtown?

What street do I turn at?

What street do I turn on?

Which exit do I get off on?

> *exit* = *expressway interchange*

What floor is your office on?

Which building is your office in?

What street is your office on?

What major streets is that between?

What major intersection is that near?

What suburb is that in?

716 Asking about transportation to a particular place

Does a bus go there?

Which bus line goes to the railway station?

What bus line goes by there?

Does a train go there?

Which train line goes to Omaha?

What train stop is that nearest?

Can you tell me what stop to get off at?

Where do I get off?

How difficult would it be to get a taxi?

Does the expressway go by there?

717 Describing a place that is difficult to find

It's in the middle of nowhere. (*idiomatic*)

It's off the beaten track. (*idiomatic*)

It's well off the beaten track. (*idiomatic*)

It's way off the beaten track. (*idiomatic*)

It's out in the boonies. (*informal*)

> *the boonies* = *the boondocks* = *the suburban areas
> that are far from the center of town*

You can't get there from here. (*cliché*)

718 Describing a place that is quite distant

It's not within walking distance.

It's a ways away.

It's quite a way(s).

You've got a way(s) to go yet.

You've got a long way to go.

719 Describing a place that is a long way away

It's a half hour drive from here.

It's a good distance. (*informal*)

It's a good ten miles (from here).

720 Describing a place that is not too far away

It's up the pike.

It's two miles up the pike.

It's two miles down the highway.

It's up the road.

It's just up the road.

It's just up the road a piece. (*folksy*)

It's down the road a piece. (*folksy*)

It's down the road a pike. (*folksy*)

It's down the road a stretch. (*folksy*)

It's a mile away, as the crow flies. (*folksy*)

It's a stone's throw away. (*cliché*)

It's just a stone's throw from here. (*cliché*)

It's within spitting distance. (*folksy*)

It's in this neck of the woods. (*folksy*)

You can see it on the horizon.

It's up ahead on the left side of the road.

It's up ahead on the left.

It's on your left.

It's two doors past the post office.

It's just around the corner.

It's just around the bend.

721 Giving specific instructions on how to get to somewhere

Turn right at the next corner.

Turn left at the corner.

Stay left at the fork in the road.

Stay to your left.

Turn around and go back a mile.

Go straight ahead through the intersection.

Cross the street.

Cross the bridge.

Head uptown and turn at the First National Bank.

Head downtown and it's just before the park.

When you get to the lake, go north.

When you get to the river, go south.

Go through three lights and turn right at the fourth.

After the stop sign, turn in the next driveway.

Keep going till you pass the church, and then go left.

Keep walking and look for a bright red neon sign.

If you reach Main Street, you've gone too far.

It's next door.

They moved up the street a mile.

It's on the next block.

Just follow the signs.

You can't miss it.

Go up the stairs and knock on the third door on your left.

Take the elevator to the fourth floor and it'll be on your right.

Take the middle bank of elevators.

Go to the lobby and ask the clerk at the desk.

Go to the lobby and call up on the house phone.

722 Advising the driver of a car

Watch out!

Look out!

Slow down.

Turn here.

You missed your turn.

You missed the turn.

You missed your exit.

You missed the exit.

I think we're lost.

Why don't you stop and ask for directions?

Keep both hands on the wheel.

I hate to be a backseat driver.

723   Asking about arriving somewhere

When will we arrive?

Are we there yet?

Are we almost there?

When do we get there?

What time do you think we will get there?

724   Concerning going to the bathroom while traveling

Where is a bathroom?

Where is a toilet?

I have to go to the bathroom.

I need to answer the call of nature.

> *the call of nature = the need to go to the toilet*

Time for a pit stop.

> *a pit stop = a quick repair stop in a road race = a quick stop for the call of nature*

I need a rest stop.

> *a rest stop = a stop at a rest room*

How long can you wait?

Is it an emergency?

Why didn't you think of that before we left?

725 **Trying to get children to behave while traveling**

Settle down back there.

Stop tormenting your sister.

Do I have to tell you again to straighten up?

If I've told you once, I've told you a thousand times, stop it!

Do I have to stop this car?

Do you want to turn around and go home right now?

CAR SERVICE

726 **Greetings from a gasoline station attendant**

Yeah? (*informal*)

What can I get you?

What do you need?

How much?

Fill **'er** up? (*informal*)

    'er = her = the gas tank

Cash or credit?

727 **Making requests to a gasoline station attendant**

Please fill it up.

    it = the gas tank

Fill **'er** up. (*informal*)

    'er = her = the gas tank

Unleaded, please.

    unleaded = lead-free gasoline

High octane, please.

    high octane = premium gasoline

Premium, please.

$10 worth, please.

Can I have the keys to the bathroom?

I need a road map.

Do you have free road maps?

How much is a road map?

How do you get to the other side of the river?

How do you get to there from here?

I need an oil change.

I think my tires are low. Please check them.

Would you please check under the hood?

> *Would you ≈ Could you, Can you, Will you*

Would you have a look under the hood?

Would you check my tires?

Would you check the oil?

Would you check the shocks?

> *shocks = shock absorbers*

Would you check the battery?

Would you clean my windows?

728 **Telling a gasoline station attendant about car problems**

I need a tune-up.

It's making a funny sound under the hood.

There's something wrong with the engine.

My engine is knocking.

If I go over fifty, the car starts shaking.

My car won't start.

It won't start.

My car broke down.

It just died on me. (*informal*)

It stalled.

My battery is dead.

Can you jump-start my car?

> *to jump-start = to start one car from another car's battery*

I need a jump. (*informal*)

> *a jump = a jump-start*

729   A gasoline station attendant offering service

Can I check your tires?

Can I check your oil?

Check the oil?

Clean your windows?

Do you want the car wash with that?

You want me to check under the hood?

Want me to check your oil?

Shall I check the oil?

Shall I check your oil?

730   A gasoline station attendant pointing out problems

Your tires are low.

That left rear tire looks low.

You need an oil change.

Your shocks are shot.

   shot = ruined

You should use a higher grade of gasoline.

You really ought to get this thing tuned (up).

I can't say offhand what the problem is.

The mechanic will have to take a look at it.

Looks to me like a real problem.

I'll have to take it into the shop.

There's a $30 charge just to look at the problem, but it'll
   go toward the cost of repair.

I'll get the tow truck out there.

Call me tomorrow and I'll give you an estimate.

You can pick it up on Friday.

731   Running out of gasoline

I've run out of gas.

I'm out of gas.

Can you sell me a gallon of gas and loan me a can to
   carry it in?

It's out of gas.

No gas.

732 Tire problems

I have a flat tire.

I have a flat.

My tire blew out.

There is a slow leak in one of the tires.

Could you please inflate my tires?

733 Problems on the highway

I need a tow truck.

I need a tow.

My car is a mile away.

My car is near the interchange.

Do you know what the problem is?

When can you give me an estimate?

When will it be ready?

734 When someone is arrested

I didn't see a stop sign.

I was only five (miles) over the limit. (*informal*)

What charge are you taking me in on?

What am I charged with?

I demand to see my lawyer.

You can't arrest me!

What's the charge?

What's the rap? (*slang*)

What's the beef? (*slang*)

I didn't do anything.

I didn't do anything wrong.

735 When a police officer stops a driver

Can I see your license?

Let me see your license. (*informal*)

Gimme your license. (*informal*)

Do you have proof of insurance?

Let me see your registration.

Do you have any idea how fast you were going?

Does this thing have a speedometer? (*sarcastic*)

Did you know you were going forty miles per hour in a thirty-mile-an-hour zone?

Where's the fire, buddy? (*informal*)

   = *If you are hurrying to a fire, where is it?*

Where's the fire, lady? (*informal*)

Do you know why I stopped you?

Do you have any idea why I stopped you?

I'm just going to give you a warning this time.

I'll let you off with a warning this time.

I'll let you go this time, but don't let it happen again.

Slow down.

If I ever catch you again, I'm taking you in.

   taking you in = taking you to the police station

I'm taking you downtown.

   downtown = police headquarters

736 Trying to intimidate a police officer — (not recommended)

What's your badge number?

I'll report you for this.

Do you know who I am?

Do you know who you are talking to?

I've got friends in the police department.

I've got friends downtown.

   downtown = police headquarters

I know people in city hall.

I have friends in high places.

GOOD-BYES AND HELLOS

737 **When someone is leaving on a journey**

Bon voyage!

Have a good trip!

Have a nice flight.

Have a nice trip.

Have a safe trip.

Have a safe journey.

Drive carefully.

Take care of yourself.

Take care.

We'll miss you.

All the best.

738 **Welcoming someone who has returned**

Welcome back!

Welcome back, stranger!

Long time no see! (*cliché*)

Where were you?

Where have you been?

Where did you go?

739 **Concerning a journey or vacation**

How was it?

How did it go?

Did everything go OK?

Did you have fun?

You'll have to tell us all about it.

Did you take any pictures?

Do you have pictures?

Were the locals friendly?

Were the natives friendly?

Did you bring me anything?
We missed you.
We missed you around here.
We've missed you around here.
It just wasn't the same without you.

LODGING

HOTELS

740 **A hotel desk clerk greeting a guest**

May I help you?

How can I serve you? (*formal*)

(A) room for how many?

How many people?

How many beds?

How many are in your group?

How many are in your party?

    party = group

How long will you be staying?

How long will you be with us?

How many nights will you be staying?

Do you have a reservation?

I'm sorry, there's no vacancy.

You will have to wait until your room is ready.

Do you mind waiting while your room is being readied?

741 **Requesting a room for one at a hotel**

I need a room, please.

I'd like a single.

Do you have any singles?

I need a room with a single bed.

I need a room for the night.

Do you have any vacancies?

Do you have a single available?

A double please.

It has to be a nonsmoking room.

A room with a bath, please.

Can I reserve a room?
Can I book a room?
I have a reservation.
Do you have a reservation for Smith?

742   Requesting a larger room at a hotel

I'd like a double.

> *a double = a room for two; a room with a double bed*

Double occupancy.

> *= Two in a room.*

Do you have a room with two double beds?
I need a room for two.
I need a room with two single beds.
I need a room with a double bed.
I'd like a room with a king(-sized bed).
I'd like a room with a queen(-sized bed).
We will need a crib for the baby.
Can we get a rollaway (bed) for the two children?

743   A hotel desk clerk finding out a guest's preferences

Would you like a room with a view of the (swimming) pool?
Would you like a smoking or a nonsmoking room?
All of our rooms have bath or shower.
Would you prefer a nonsmoking room?
Smoking or nonsmoking?
Smoking or non?

744   Special requests at a hotel

I'd like a room at the front.

> *I'd like ≈ I need, I'll need, Do you have (?), Can I have (?)*

I'd like a room at the rear.
I'd like the quietest room you have.

I'd like a room with a view of the city.

I'd like a suite.

I'd like a room for the week.

I'd like a wake-up call, please.

I'm staying the weekend.

745 Questions asked of a hotel clerk

Does that have a shower?

Where is the ice machine?

Are there vending machines available?

Do you have a pool?

Where is the pool, please?

Is there a pool?

Do you have a fax machine available?

What are the rates?

How much is this room?

Do you serve meals?

Is there a restaurant?

How do I get room service?

Are pets allowed?

746 Checking out of a hotel

When do I have to be out of the room by?

What time is checkout?

When's checkout?

Is there a penalty for late checkout?

I need to check out.

Please have my luggage brought down.

Please call me a taxi.

747 Asking about payment at a hotel

Do you take credit cards?

The bill, please.

I'd like a receipt, please.

748   Listing the special rules at a hotel

No pets allowed.

The pool closes at midnight.

The restaurant is open until 11 p.m.

The restaurant is located just off the lobby.

You'll find the restaurant just around the corner.

Checkout (time) is (at) 11 a.m.

749   Completing the hotel check-in

Here is your key.

Do you need a bellboy?

I'll have someone bring your luggage up.

I'll have someone bring your baggage up.

Your luggage will be there shortly.

Enjoy your stay.

ROOMS AND APARTMENTS

750   Requesting rooms from a rental agent

I'm looking for a studio (apartment).

> *I'm looking for ≈ Do you have (?), I'd like to rent, I need, I want, I'd prefer*

I'm looking for an efficiency.

> *an efficiency = a one-room apartment*

I'm looking for a one-bedroom (apartment).

I'm looking for a two-bedroom.

I'd like a view of the lake.

I'd like a view of the ocean.

751   General questions for a rental agent

What's the rent?

How much is the rent?

What floor is it on?

Is there a security system?

Are smoke detectors provided?

Are utilities included?
>   *utilities* = *the cost of heat, water, and electricity*

Does that include utilities?

How much does the electricity usually cost a month?

Do you require a deposit?

Do you require a security deposit?

What kind of neighborhood is it?

Is it safe to walk at night?

Is there a storage area in the basement?

Is this an elevator building?

Is this a quiet neighborhood?

Does the building have a security system?

Does the building have security?

Does the building have an attendant?

Can I see the place now?

Is there a laundry available?

Are laundry machines available?

Is a washer and dryer available?

When can I take occupancy? (*formal*)

When can I move in?

752   Questions about the convenience of transportation

Is it close to public transportation?
>   *it* = *lodging you propose to rent*

How far from the bus is it?

How close to the subway is it?

Is it near the train?

753   Questions about rules in rental lodging

Can I bring pets?

Are pets OK?

Are pets allowed?

Are children allowed?

Are waterbeds permitted?

754 A rental agent's statements about the payment of rent

We require the first and last months' rent and a security deposit up front.

The security deposit is a month-and-a-half's rent.

Rent is due by the fifth of the month.

If your rent comes in past the fifth, a late charge will be added.

755 Additional costs in the rental of lodgings

All utilities are included.

   utilities = the cost of gas, heat, and electricity

Utilities aren't included.

You have to pay for electricity.

   You have to ≈ You must, You will, You are required

You have to pay your own electric.

You have to pay gas.

You have to pay heat.

You have to pay electricity.

Rent doesn't include gas.

756 Special information about lodgings

There's a laundry in the basement.

There's a laundromat across the street.

   laundromat = a commercial do-it-yourself laundry

The units come with a washer and dryer.

Each unit has its own air-conditioning.

Each unit is centrally air-conditioned.

Each unit has a window air-conditioner.

The unit is air-conditioned.

Garbage is collected on Wednesday.

The trash collector comes on Wednesday.

Each unit has a trash compactor.

The incinerator chute is at the end of the hall.

You can move in immediately.

It's available for immediate occupancy.

It's available on the first of the month.

There is an attendant on duty 24 hours in the lobby.

We have no studios available.

What is your price range?

Sign here, please.

757   Describing the availability of transportation

It's two blocks from the subway.

> *it = the lodging you propose to rent*

It's two blocks from the bus.

It's near transportation.

There is a long walk to the train.

758   Special rules for rooms and apartments

No children.

No pets.

You can have tropical fish.

No waterbeds.

Cats only.

Dogs only.

759   Complaining about lodgings

It's too cold.

It's too hot.

There's no heat.

The heat is out.

The furnace is out.

The electricity isn't working.

The roof is leaking.

The roof leaks.

The toilet is running.

The toilet runs all the time.

The sink is backed up.

The sink is clogged.

One of the windows is broken.

The storm windows need to be put in.

760 **Responding to a tenant's complaints about lodgings**

Here's the name and phone number of the superintendent.

I'll have someone out (there) Monday to fix it.

The exterminator is coming on Tuesday, so remove
everything from your kitchen shelves.

761 **Concerning payment of rent**

I'm going to be a little late with the rent.

Your rent is due.

Your rent is past due.

If you don't pay by this Friday, you're out.

That will come out of your security deposit.

Your rent is always late.

EMERGENCIES

ACCIDENTS

762 **Asking what has happened at the scene of an accident**

What happened?

How did it happen?

What's going on here?

Are they going to be OK?

Has the family been notified?

763 **Asking for help at the scene of an accident**

Is there a doctor here?

Can you help stop the bleeding?

Does anyone know CPR?

> *CPR = cardiopulmonary resuscitation*

Do you know how to apply a tourniquet?

Call 911.

Call the police.

Call an ambulance.

Get the paramedics.

Get some help.

Get a doctor quick.

764 **Dealing with an injured person at the scene of an accident**

Is he breathing?

Get some blankets.

Get a first-aid kit.

We need some bandages.

Stop the flow of blood.

Apply pressure to stem the flow of blood.

Elevate his legs.

Raise his legs.

Elevate the arm.

Keep him quiet.

Don't move him.

Don't move.

Stay right there.

Stay put.

765   Asking someone about injuries received in an accident

Are you OK?

Are you all right?

Are you hurt?

Where does it hurt?

Can you move your arm?

766   Explaining that you have witnessed an accident

I saw the whole thing.

I'm a witness.

I witnessed it.

I can provide a description of the car.

I can provide a description of the assailant.

    the assailant = the attacker

I got the license plate number.

I got the license number of the car.

USING 911, THE EMERGENCY TELEPHONE NUMBER

767   Emergency telephone calls

I want to report a fire.

My house has been robbed!

A water main has burst out in the street.

My uncle is having chest pains and we need the
  paramedics.

I want to report a robbery in progress.

There is a house on fire at 406 Maple Street.

There's been an accident, and we need an ambulance.

This is an emergency.

I need the police.

Please connect me with the police.

Get me the police.

THE LIFE AND DEATH EMERGENCY

768 Life and death emergencies — fire

There's someone in that house!

My baby is asleep in there!

Save my cat!

Please try to find my brother!

769 Life and death emergencies — violence

He hit me!

She pulled a gun on me!

I got stabbed in the side.

I've been shot.

They beat my brother, and he is bleeding badly.

770 Life and death emergencies — accidents

My cousin fell off a ladder!

A car hit her and broke her back!

My child has been run over.

They drove by and shot my son.

771 Life and death emergencies — medical

My baby has stopped breathing.

I'm having terrible chest pains.

I cut myself on broken glass, and I am bleeding very badly.

I think my leg is broken.

Help, I've fallen and I can't get up!

THE POLICE

772 Requests for help from a police officer

Help!

Please help me!

This is an emergency!

Please come quick. Someone is hurt! (*informal*)

Excuse me, officer, can you help me?

I seem to be lost.

I've locked my keys in my car.

Can you help me get the keys out of my car?

My car is missing.

My car has been stolen.

I've been robbed.

I've been mugged.

I've been raped.

He has a gun.

We're trapped up here.

We're trapped in here.

There's someone trying to get into my house.

773 A police officer seeking information

What seems to be the problem here?

Tell me exactly what happened.

Are you lost?

Can you provide a description of the missing person?

Can you describe the assailant? (*formal*)
> the assailant = the attacker

Do you have a permit to do that?

What's going on here?

774 A police officer confronting a criminal

Freeze! Police!

Hands up!

Put your hands up!

Put your hands on your head.

Take your hands out of your pockets slowly.

Turn around slowly.

Step out of the car slowly.

Break it up, you guys. (*informal*)

You're under arrest.

I'm taking you in.

You have the right to remain silent.

Tell it to a lawyer! (*informal*)

Tell it to the judge!

I don't care who you are!

Using the Word and Concept Index

The Word and Concept Index enables the user to locate expressions relating to a specific topic by looking under a key word or a key concept in the topic itself. A topic number, rather than a page number, is provided at the end of each topic description, indicating where to find that topic in the list of expressions.

For instance, if you were looking for something to do with headaches, you would look under **HEAD** or **PAIN** where you would find the expression group "Describing a pain in the head ▶ **488.**" Look for "Describing a pain in the head" at number 488 in the list of expressions.

Word and
Concept Index

Advising the driver of a car ► 722
Medical warnings and advice found on product labels ► 514
Offering someone help and advice ► 274

AFFAIRS
Asking someone to stay out of your affairs ► 187

AGENTS
A newspaper agent responding to complaints ► 598
A rental agent's statements about the payment of rent ► 754
Expressions used with a newspaper agent ► 596
General questions for a rental agent ► 751
Making a complaint to a newspaper agent ► 595
Questions a passenger might ask of an airline ticket agent ► 678
Questions asked by a ticket agent for an entertainment event ► 587
Questions asked by a travel agent ► 673
Requesting a subscription from a magazine agent ► 594
Requesting rooms from a rental agent ► 750
Requests made to a ticket agent ► 584
Requests made to a travel agent ► 674
Responses from a magazine agent ► 597

AGGRESSIVENESS
Encouraging someone to be less aggressive — informal ► 86

AGREEING
Agreeing with a speaker ► 51
Simple agreement ► 25
Stating your concurrence ► 26
Agreeing to something — polite ► 137

AIRLINES
Announcing changes in an airline flight ► 682
Describing types of airline flights ► 677
Questions a passenger might ask about an airline flight ► 676
Questions a passenger might ask of an airline ticket agent ► 678
Rescheduling an airline flight ► 679

AIRPLANES
Eating and drinking on an airplane ► 686
On an airplane ► 685
When an airplane is crowded ► 683

AIRPORTS
At the airport boarding gate ► 684

ALCOHOL
A bartender asking what you want ► 443
Asking for a small drink of beverage alcohol ► 452
Asking what's available at a bar ► 444
Buying beverage alcohol at a supermarket ► 392

BEER
Requesting a glass or bottle of beer ▶ **445**

BEHAVIOR
Asking a child to stop some behavior ▶ **352**
Trying to get children to behave while traveling ▶ **725**
When a parent is frustrated with a child's behavior ▶ **362**

BELIEVING
Concerning vision and belief ▶ **305**
Encouraging someone to believe you ▶ **104**

BEVERAGES
Asking for a small drink of beverage alcohol ▶ **452**
Buying beverage alcohol at a supermarket ▶ **392**

BICKERING
When children bicker ▶ **345**

BILLS
A teller inquiring about the size of bills that you want ▶ **376**
Asking for the bill in a restaurant ▶ **440**
Concerning the payment of a bill in a restaurant ▶ **442**
Requesting large or small bills when cashing a check ▶ **367**

BIT
Offering someone a bit of food ▶ **467**

BLACKNESS
Concerning blackness ▶ **256**

BLAMING
Accepting the blame for something ▶ **147**
Admitting your errors ▶ **148**
Blaming something on fate or destiny ▶ **112**

BLEEDING
Telling the doctor about bleeding ▶ **498**

BOARDING
At the airport boarding gate ▶ **684**
General questions when boarding a bus ▶ **696**
Instructions when boarding a bus ▶ **702**

BOOKS
A library desk clerk's responses ▶ **622**
At the service counter of a library ▶ **621**
Questions for a librarian ▶ **620**

BOTHERSOME
Apologizing to someone you have bothered ▶ **135**
Describing a bothersome person ▶ **178**
Inviting an annoying person to leave ▶ **173**

CABS
(See *TAXIS* in this index.)

CAFÉS
Expressions used to make friends at a bar or café ▶ 56
Ordering drinks at a café ▶ 407
Placing an order in a café ▶ 405
Special instructions at a café ▶ 406

CALLER
Asking whom a telephone caller wants to talk to ▶ 647
Connecting or transferring a telephone caller ▶ 649
Offering to help a telephone caller ▶ 654
Offering to take a message from a telephone caller ▶ 653
Putting a telephone caller on hold ▶ 650

CALLING
Calling someone crazy ▶ 92
Bringing a telephone call to an end ▶ 655
Emergency telephone calls ▶ 767
Interrupting a telephone call with other business ▶ 651
Making complaints about unwanted telephone calls ▶ 659
Making emergency calls ▶ 658
Screening someone's telephone calls ▶ 648
Taking a call off hold ▶ 652

CARE
Encouraging someone to be prudent — clichés ▶ 69
Caring for pets ▶ 334
Employer to lawn-care worker ▶ 642
Explaining that you are receiving medical care ▶ 511
Instructions to lawn-care worker ▶ 643
Lawn-care worker to employer ▶ 644
Offering care to a sick person ▶ 491

CAREFREE
When someone is carefree ▶ 282

CARPETING
Concerning furniture or carpeting ▶ 326

CARS
(See *AUTOMOBILES* in this index.)

CASHIER
Requesting change from a teller or cashier ▶ 368

CASHING
Requesting large or small bills when cashing a check ▶ 367

CURED
Explaining that you are cured of a health problem ▶ 512

CUSTOMERS
A postal clerk greeting a customer ▶ 575
A salesperson greeting a customer ▶ 554
A salesperson offering help to a customer ▶ 555
An automobile dealer greeting a customer ▶ 599
Encouraging remarks a salesperson might make to a customer ▶ 565
Offering additional help to a customer ▶ 558
Offering merchandise to a customer ▶ 557
Questions a customer might ask in a store ▶ 563
Questions a florist might ask a customer ▶ 592
Questions a postal clerk might ask a customer ▶ 579
Questions a salesperson might ask a customer ▶ 556
Questions asked of a restaurant customer ▶ 421
When a customer wants to try on clothing ▶ 564

CUSTOMS
Entering the United States through customs and immigration ▶ 687

DAMAGED
Complaining about lost or damaged luggage ▶ 680

DANCING
Inviting someone to dance ▶ 57

DATING
Asking someone for a date ▶ 306

DAYS
Greetings for various times of the day ▶ 3
Asking the time of day ▶ 123
Reciting special meal offers for the day ▶ 419

DEADLINE
Approaching a deadline ▶ 538

DEALERS
An automobile dealer finding out what you want ▶ 600
An automobile dealer greeting a customer ▶ 599

DEALING
Dealing with an injured person at the scene of an accident ▶ 764

DEATH
Expressing death ▶ 237
Life and death emergencies — accidents ▶ 770
Life and death emergencies — fire ▶ 768
Life and death emergencies — medical ▶ 771
Life and death emergencies — violence ▶ 769

EXCUSING
Asking to leave the dinner table early ► **323**
Excuses for failure or offense ► **536**
Excusing oneself from the table ► **473**

EXHAUSTED
Describing being exhausted or worn-out ► **490**

EXHIBITING
Showing disbelief ► **108**

EXPECTATION
Concerning expectation ► **259**

EXPENSES
Controlling expenses ► **379**

EXPERIENCE
Describing a lack of work experience ► **528**

EXTRA
Making an extra effort ► **262**

EYES
Allergic problems with the eyes ► **483**

FACTS
Arguing about the facts ► **37**
Knowing something after the fact ► **113**

FAILURE
Excuses for failure or offense ► **536**

FAMILIES
Describing family relationships ► **314**
Family solidarity ► **315**

FAR
Describing a place that is not too far away ► **720**

FARES
Asking about bus and subway fare ► **695**
Paying a taxi fare ► **711**

FAST
Concerning speed in a taxi ► **707**

FAST-FOOD
A fast-food clerk asking where the food will be eaten ► **396**
A fast-food clerk delivering an order ► **402**
A fast-food clerk offering food items ► **401**
A fast-food clerk taking an order ► **395**
Complaining about a fast-food order ► **403**
Ordering drinks at a fast-food restaurant ► **398**
Placing an order for fast-food products ► **397**

HARM
Complaining about lost or damaged luggage ► **680**
Excuses for failure or offense ► **536**
Statements about sexual and physical abuse ► **518**

HARSH
Explaining harsh justice ► **196**

HEAD
Describing a pain in the head ► **488**

HEARING
Concerning ears or hearing ► **296**
Difficulty in hearing ► **293**
Hearing loud and soft sounds ► **295**
Lacking an ear for music ► **294**

HEAT
Concerning the temperature in a taxi ► **709**
Feeling warm or hot ► **252**

HEATER
Describing plumbing problems — water heater ► **629**

HELP
When you are helpless to help — rude ► **204**

HELPING
Giving advice to someone whose life is too busy ► **70**
Offering help to someone ► **61**
A salesperson offering help to a customer ► **555**
Advising the driver of a car ► **722**
Asking for help at the scene of an accident ► **763**
Asking someone about injuries received in an accident ► **765**
Dealing with an injured person at the scene of an accident ► **764**
Explaining that you will attend to someone soon ► **138**
Expressions used by a telephone directory assistance operator ► **662**
Offering additional help to a customer ► **558**
Offering care to a sick person ► **491**
Offering merchandise to a customer ► **557**
Offering someone help and advice ► **274**
Offering to help a telephone caller ► **654**
Requesting a telephone number from directory assistance ► **656**
Requests for help from a police officer ► **772**
Statements made to a guidance counselor or therapist ► **516**
Statements made to a marriage counselor ► **519**

HELPLESS
When you are helpless to help — rude ► **204**

HIGHWAY
Problems on the highway ► **733**

MESSAGES
Offering to take a message from a telephone caller ► 653
Recorded telephone service messages ► 665

MESSY
Describing a messy place ► 247
Observing that someone looks disorderly ► 476

MILD
Expressing mild discomfort owing to illness ► 486

MILEAGE
Asking about frequent flyer mileage ► 681

MINGLING
Mingling with other guests ► 220

MINUTES
The time is fifteen minutes past the hour ► 128
The time is fifty minutes past the hour ► 131
The time is forty-five minutes past the hour ► 130
The time is forty minutes past the hour ► 129
The time is ten minutes past the hour ► 127

MISCELLANEOUS
Miscellaneous expressions used by a postal clerk ► 580

MISTAKES
Attempting to put an end to a misunderstanding ► 103
Criticizing someone's misunderstanding ► 102
Promising never to repeat a particular mistake ► 149

MISUNDERSTANDINGS
Attempting to put an end to a misunderstanding ► 103
Criticizing someone's misunderstanding ► 102

MOCK
Expressing mock sympathy ► 202
Expressing mock sympathy — sarcastic ► 203

MONEY
When someone is in debt ► 79
When you are out of money ► 78
A bank teller greeting a patron ► 365
A barber or hairdresser asking for payment ► 637
A clerk asking about payment ► 390
A clerk asking about prices ► 389
A rental agent's statements about the payment of rent ► 754
A taxi driver discussing payment ► 712
A teller inquiring about the size of bills that you want ► 376
About payment for a meal in a restaurant ► 441

MORE

Requesting additional information from a telephone solicitor ► **671**
Requesting additional servings in a restaurant ► **430**

MOTIONS
Concerning motions under parliamentary procedure ► **543**

MOVING
Steering a guest to a particular room ► **218**
When your moving about may bother someone ► **133**

MUCH
When you are overworked and doing too much ► **81**
When someone argues too much ► **171**
When someone drinks too much ► **457**

MUSIC
Lacking an ear for music ► **294**

NAME
Expressions for a forgotten word or name ► **245**

NAP
Taking a nap ► **330**

NEEDLESS
Requesting someone to stop needless talk ► **199**

NEGOTIATING
Expressions heard in negotiating sessions ► **545**

NEW
Asking about a new baby ► **160**
Beginning a new project or activity ► **546**
Choosing a new car's options ► **602**
Explaining why you are having difficulty in a new job ► **535**
Seeing a new baby ► **159**

NEWSPAPERS
A newspaper agent responding to complaints ► **598**
Expressions used with a newspaper agent ► **596**
Making a complaint to a newspaper agent ► **595**
Requesting a publication from a news vendor ► **593**

NOSE
Allergic problems with the nose and breathing ► **481**

NOSTALGIA
Concerning nostalgia ► **249**

NOTING
Noting digressions in a conversation ► **48**

NUMBER
Requesting a telephone number from directory assistance ► **656**

OPERATION
Asking about computer operation ▶ 615

OPERATORS
Expressions used by a telephone directory assistance operator ▶ 662
Expressions used by a telephone repair service operator ▶ 663
Requests to a telephone operator ▶ 657

OPINIONS
Asking for a diner's opinion of a meal ▶ 437
When someone interrupts with an opinion ▶ 192

OPPOSITE SEX
Approaching the opposite sex ▶ 58

OPTIONS
Choosing a new car's options ▶ 602

ORDER
Regarding order and procedure ▶ 246
When something is out of order ▶ 270

ORDERING
A fast-food clerk delivering an order ▶ 402
A fast-food clerk taking an order ▶ 395
Asking about payment for goods ordered over the telephone ▶ 669
Asking how to place a merchandise order over the telephone ▶ 668
Complaining about a fast-food order ▶ 403
Concerning food allergies when ordering at a restaurant ▶ 428
Explaining to a waiter or waitress that you are not ready to order ▶ 424
Indicating readiness to order a meal at a restaurant ▶ 425
Ordering drinks at a café ▶ 407
Ordering drinks at a fast-food restaurant ▶ 398
Ordering flowers from a florist ▶ 591
Ordering food to be taken out ▶ 434
Ordering wine in a restaurant ▶ 431
Placing a telephone order for pizza ▶ 409
Placing an order at a bakery for something to drink ▶ 460
Placing an order for baked goods ▶ 459
Placing an order for fast-food products ▶ 397
Placing an order in a café ▶ 405
Placing an order with a dry cleaner or a launderer ▶ 616
Special orders in a bakery ▶ 462
Taking out a bakery order or eating it in the shop ▶ 461
Taking your order ▶ 404
Taking your order for a pizza ▶ 408
Telling where a fast-food order will be eaten ▶ 400

Explaining that you are cured of a health problem ▶ **512**
Explaining why you are having difficulty in a new job ▶ **535**
Problems on the highway ▶ **733**
Reporting problems to a utility company ▶ **631**
Telling a gasoline station attendant about car problems ▶ **728**
Telling the doctor about bowel problems ▶ **502**
Telling the doctor about sleep problems ▶ **503**
Telling the doctor about various pains and problems ▶ **499**
Tire problems ▶ **732**

PROCEDURES
Adjourning a meeting under parliamentary procedure ▶ **544**
Concerning motions under parliamentary procedure ▶ **543**
Expressions used under parliamentary procedure ▶ **542**
Regarding order and procedure ▶ **246**

PRODUCTS
Health claims found on consumer products ▶ **515**
Medical warnings and advice found on product labels ▶ **514**
Placing an order for fast-food products ▶ **397**

PROFESSING
Professing love ▶ **308**

PROFESSOR
Questioning a college professor ▶ **338**

PROJECTS
Beginning a new project or activity ▶ **546**
Ending a project ▶ **551**
Starting over again on a project ▶ **552**

PROMISING
Promising to keep a secret ▶ **74**
Promising never to repeat a particular mistake ▶ **149**

PROPERTY
Asking someone to leave your property alone ▶ **186**

PROPOSITION
Stating your disagreement with a proposition ▶ **33**

PROSPECTIVE
A prospective employee to a human resources or personnel director
▶ **525**
A prospective employee to a prospective employer during an interview
▶ **523**
An employer to a prospective employee during an interview ▶ **524**

PROVIDING
When a salesperson cannot supply exactly what is wanted ▶ **567**

PRUDENT
Encouraging someone to be prudent — clichés ► 69

PUBLIC
Asking about the location of a rest room in a public building ► 433

PUBLICATION
Requesting a publication from a news vendor ► 593

PUNISHMENT
When punishment is in store for someone ► 195

PURCHASES
Asking how a purchase will be paid for ► 566
Buying beverage alcohol at a supermarket ► 392
Getting a purchase gift wrapped in a store ► 570
Getting grocery store purchases to the car ► 394
Health claims found on consumer products ► 515
Placing an order for fast-food products ► 397
Requesting a subscription from a magazine agent ► 594
Requesting instructions for packing your purchases ► 386

PUSHED
On being pushed to the limit of your patience ► 271

PUTTING
Attempting to put an end to a misunderstanding ► 103
Putting a telephone caller on hold ► 650

QUIET
Encouraging a child to be quiet ► 351
Requesting silence ► 198

QUITE
Describing a place that is quite distant ► 718

RADIO
Concerning a radio or stereo ► 325

RATES
Information about foreign exchange rates ► 374

REACH
Telling a babysitter how to reach you ► 608

READINESS
Asking when a meal will be ready ► 464
Explaining to a waiter or waitress that you are not ready to order ► 424
Getting ready to study or do homework ► 335
Indicating readiness to order a meal at a restaurant ► 425
Stating when food will be ready ► 466

SERVED
Requesting that certain foods not be served to you in a restaurant ► **427**

SERVICES
A dry cleaner or launderer offering services ► **617**
A gasoline station attendant offering service ► **729**
A waiter or waitress seeking to be of further service ► **438**
Asking questions at the grocery store service counter ► **393**
At the service counter of a library ► **621**
Expressions used by a telephone repair service operator ► **663**
Recorded telephone service messages ► **665**
Requesting service from a utility company by telephone ► **630**
Requesting telephone service or installation ► **661**

SERVINGS
Concerning additional servings of food ► **470**
Requesting additional servings in a restaurant ► **430**
Second servings ► **320**

SESSIONS
Expressions heard in negotiating sessions ► **545**

SETTING UP
Arranging for a babysitter ► **606**

SETTLED
Stating that something is settled ► **106**

SEX
Concerning pregnancy ► **310**
Concerning romantic or sexual attraction ► **307**
Sexual expressions ► **311**
Sexually phrased insults and retorts ► **312**
Statements about sexual and physical abuse ► **518**

SHOCK
Asking in disbelief or disagreement ► **96**
Showing disbelief ► **108**
When someone has been insolent or rude — shocked response ► **166**

SHOES
Instructions for a shoe repair clerk ► **571**

SHOP
Taking out a bakery order or eating it in the shop ► **461**

SHOPPING
A clerk asking about prices ► **389**
An automobile dealer finding out what you want ► **600**
Asking about payment at a grocery store ► **385**

SILENCE
Encouraging a child to be quiet ▶ 351
Requesting silence ▶ 198

SIMILARITIES
Commenting on personal similarities ▶ 55

SIMPLE
Simple greetings ▶ 1
Simple agreement ▶ 25
Simple good-byes ▶ 21
Stating simple disagreement or refusal ▶ 30
Simple forgiveness ▶ 152

SINCERE
Sincere apologies ▶ 145

SINKS
Describing plumbing problems — sinks ▶ 625

SITTING
Asking about a bus seat you want to sit in ▶ 694
Asking about a train seat you want to sit in ▶ 690

SITUATION
Making the best of a bad situation ▶ 111

SIZE
A teller inquiring about the size of bills that you want ▶ 376
Requesting a larger room at a hotel ▶ 742

SKIN
Allergic problems with the skin ▶ 484

SLEEPING
Going to bed and to sleep ▶ 331
Instructions to a babysitter about feeding and bedtime ▶ 611
Sending a child to bed ▶ 361
Telling the doctor about sleep problems ▶ 503

SLOWLY
Encouraging someone to be patient and take things slowly ▶ 68

SMALL
Asking for a small drink of beverage alcohol ▶ 452
Offering someone a small portion of food ▶ 298
Praising a small child ▶ 349
Requesting large or small bills when cashing a check ▶ 367

SMELLING
Identifying smells ▶ 300

SMOKING
A smoker's response to a nonsmoker's complaint ▶ 89

VERIFYING
Verifying your route when traveling ▶ 714

VERY
Describing a place that is quite distant ▶ 718
Offering a very polite apology ▶ 146
When someone is very annoying or hurtful ▶ 174
When someone is very happy — idioms ▶ 279
When someone looks very bad ▶ 477
When someone looks very happy ▶ 278

VIEWING
Giving a child instructions for television watching ▶ 358

VIOLENCE
Life and death emergencies — violence ▶ 769

VISION
Concerning good vision ▶ 304
Concerning vision and belief ▶ 305
Difficulties with seeing ▶ 303

VISIT
Asking to visit someone ▶ 205

VISITATION
Expressing sympathy at a funeral or wake ▶ 163

VISITORS
After greeting a visitor ▶ 213
Greetings for visitors ▶ 211
Inviting a visitor to come in ▶ 212
Inviting a visitor to stay for dinner ▶ 215
Making a visitor feel welcome and comfortable ▶ 214
When you do not understand what a foreign visitor has said ▶ 122

VOMITING
Telling the doctor about vomiting ▶ 501
When you feel like vomiting ▶ 487

WAITERS
A waiter or waitress offering dessert ▶ 439
A waiter or waitress seeking to be of further service ▶ 438
Explaining to a waiter or waitress that you are not ready to order
▶ 424
Greetings from a waiter or waitress ▶ 417
Questions a waiter or waitress might ask ▶ 418
Requesting attention from a waiter or waitress ▶ 423

WAITING
Asking someone to wait ▶ 67
Asking a taxi driver to wait ▶ 710

WELCOMING
Making a visitor feel welcome and comfortable ▶ 214
Welcoming someone who has returned ▶ 738

WELLNESS
Explaining that you are cured of a health problem ▶ 512
Inquiring about someone's health or well-being ▶ 478
Starting a conversation with someone you know well ▶ 224
When someone does not look well ▶ 479
Wishing someone well ▶ 162

WHITENESS
Concerning whiteness ▶ 255

WHY
Asking why someone looks so unhappy ▶ 273
Explaining why one is late ▶ 209
Explaining why you are having difficulty in a new job ▶ 535
Explaining why you are not going to do something ▶ 537

WINE
Ordering wine in a restaurant ▶ 431

WISDOM
Encouraging someone to be more sensible ▶ 95

WISHING
Returning someone's good wishes ▶ 136
Wishing someone well ▶ 162

WITNESSING
Explaining that you have witnessed an accident ▶ 766

WORD
Expressions for a forgotten word or name ▶ 245

WORK
A prospective employee to a human resources or personnel director ▶ 525
A prospective employee to a prospective employer during an interview ▶ 523
An employee to a human resources or personnel director ▶ 526
An employer to a prospective employee during an interview ▶ 524
Complaining to a human resources or personnel director ▶ 527
Concerning an easy task or employment position ▶ 529
Concerning being busy — clichés ▶ 261
Congratulating someone for doing a good job ▶ 161
Describing a lack of work experience ▶ 528
Employer to lawn-care worker ▶ 642
Encouraging someone to keep working at a job ▶ 541
Explaining why you are having difficulty in a new job ▶ 535

ABOUT THE AUTHORS

Richard A. Spears, Ph.D. is Adjunct Associate Professor of Linguistics, Northwestern University, and a specialist in lexicography, phonetics, English as a Second Language, and American culture. He is also Executive Editor of the Dictionary Department at NTC Publishing Group.

Steven R. Kleinedler holds a B.A. in linguistics from Northwestern University and is a doctoral student in the Linguistics Department at the University of Chicago.

Betty J. Birner, Ph.D. is a Postdoctoral Fellow in the Institute for Research in Cognitive Science at the University of Pennsylvania, where she is doing research on pragmatics and discourse.